**Nina Farewell**
is a pseudonym but the author has described
herself as 'flawless from head to toe ... the
eye-lashes alone have, like a magnet, drawn
men across a crowded room ... my curves are
intelligently distributed ... I am elegant enough
to intrigue the most vulgar of men, vulgar
enough to enchant the most cultured ... I am
equally appreciated by truck drivers, tradesmen,
salesmen, mesomorphs, endomorphs,
ectomorphs, artists and playboys.'

# The Unfair Sex

## NINA FAREWELL

### ILLUSTRATED BY ROY DOTY

Icon Books

This edition published in the UK in 2004
by Icon Books Ltd., The Old Dairy,
Brook Road, Thriplow,
Cambridge SG8 7RG
email: info@iconbooks.co.uk
www.iconbooks.co.uk

Originally published in 1953 by Frederick Muller Ltd.
Every effort has been made to trace the copyright holder
of the material reproduced in this book.
If notified, the publisher will be pleased to
acknowledge the use of any copyright material.

Sold in the UK, Europe, South Africa
and Asia by Faber and Faber Ltd.,
3 Queen Square, London WC1N 3AU
or their agents

Distributed in the UK, Europe, South Africa
and Asia by TBS Ltd., Frating Distribution Centre,
Colchester Road, Frating Green, Colchester CO7 7DW

Published in Australia in 2004
by Allen & Unwin Pty. Ltd.,
PO Box 8500, 83 Alexander Street,
Crows Nest, NSW 2065

Distributed in Canada by
Penguin Books Canada,
10 Alcorn Avenue, Suite 300,
Toronto, Ontario M4V 3B2

1 84046 603 0

# Contents

1. The Facts of Life                                                    9

2. False Prophets and Propaganda                                       17

3. Why a Man Wants What He Wants                                       23
   *The Sixteen Joys of Man — Petty Accusations against Women*

4. And What He Does To Get It                                          46
   *Flattery — Conversation Piece — Intrigue — The Mating Instinct*

5. Lines                                                               52
   *Don't Be a Kid — What Are You Saving It For? — Sex Is Beautiful — The Rush — Charity Drive — Sneak Preview — Where Does It Hurt? — The Bedside Manner — Supersalesman — The Scientific Approach — The Intellectual Approach — The Spiritual Approach — Like a Father to You — Mother Me — For Medicinal Purposes Only — Confidence Game — Eat, Drink and Be Merry — The Expert*

# CONTENTS

6. Devices                                                    80

*The Uniform — The Portrait — The Musicale — The Ring — The Twenty-four Carat Toy — The Troo-de-Loo*

7. Techniques                                                 88

*The Body Technique — The Dearest-Enemies Technique — The Open-Hand Technique — The Strong-Arm Technique — The Gibraltar Technique — The Liquor Technique — The Oblique Technique*

8. International Relations                                    100

9. How To Invite Aggression                                  104

*Modesty — Goodness — Tenderness — Generosity — Brightness — Charm — Mystery — Delicacy — Kindness*

10. How To Resist a Man                                      112

*Practical Suggestions for Resisting — Evasions — How To Say No If You Must*

11. The Pangs and Pains of Giving                            121

*Failure — Disappointment — Secrecy — Compromise — Humiliation — Impermanence*

12. Why Didn't I Hear from Him Again                         133

*Not in the Market — Shopping — The Fly-by-Night — Stalemate*

13. The Joys and Rewards of Refusing                         142

14. Virtue                                                   147

15. Never Go to a Man's Flat                                 152

16. How To Behave When You Get There                         158

17. How To Be Made Love To                                   163

# CONTENTS

18. How To Drop a Man without Hurting Him    168

19. How To Take the Pleasure Out of It for Him    172
   *Some Ways To Make a Man Miserable*

20. On Catching a Wealthy Sponsor    179

21. Don't Have an Affair with Your Boss    182

22. Don't Have an Affair with a Married Man    185

23. How Shall We Love Them    189

## CHAPTER ONE

# The Facts of Life

*"As soon as there is life there is danger."*—EMERSON

EVER since the author's eighteenth birthday, when she surrendered her virginity because she was afraid to seem rude, she has felt the crying need of a handbook for girls —a manual on How to Cope with Men.

The average young woman sallies forth into the world poorly equipped to face her male adversary. Too often does she find herself in a situation where she wonders what to say, how to behave, what to expect. Compulsory education provides her with a knowledge of biology, and she therefore knows about sex from the abstract or classroom point of view. But nothing is done to acquaint her with the practical problems which, from the time of her first date, confront her in all her encounters with men. Even if she finds out about hormones and chromosomes, and reads about frustrations and inhibitions, she still does not have the vaguest idea of what constitutes proper behaviour in a man's room.

People smile indulgently at the romantic games played

by young men and women in the pre-marital years, and pretend it is all very innocent and gay. The truth is known to everyone, but by common consent it is ignored—except by a few rude people like Kinsey and the late Sigmund Freud. This deliberate refusal to acknowledge the Facts of Life is responsible for the haphazard education a girl receives on so vital a subject. As a consequence, she has little chance of holding her own and succumbs to her superior adversary more often than not.

The male similarly receives no formal instruction to guide him in his behaviour with women. However, he is permitted and even expected to educate himself. Under the peculiar standards of society, boys enjoy a freedom which encourages them to start experimenting in this field at an early age, and this they do conscientiously. As they mature, they widen their sphere of experience at every opportunity and on every level. In addition, there is a freemasonry among males—an uninhibited exchange of bits of information and lessons learned, which further increases their general know-how.

Naturally, all this tends to give boys an unfair advantage over girls, an advantage which I hope to counterbalance by publicizing in these pages some hitherto carefully veiled facts. For it is my earnest contention that if a girl is going to do that which she should not, she should do it only because she *wants* to, and *not* because she was tricked into it.

In bringing this data to public attention, it is not my aim to stimulate animosity between male and female. Quite the contrary. For one of the liveliest and loveliest aspects of life is the magnetic attraction that exists between the sexes. It adds colour, excitement, music and dash to the daily routine of living. Indeed, there is something heartwarming in the thought that all over the world, every hour of the day and night, men and women are constantly seeking one another out, eager to come together and form a relationship.

But alas, one must take note that there is an important divergence, which at first glance is not apparent:

 *Each sex has a very different goal in view.*

The female is eager to cultivate the friendship of men for admirable reasons: One, to acquire a husband. Two, practically nothing that is any fun can be done without a male escort.

Men, however, do not seek feminine companionship for the pure enjoyment of conversation, dancing, picnics, marriage, and other innocent pleasures. Regrettably, they have something else in mind.

Thus we have two factions split asunder by clashing objectives, yet irresistibly drawn together by an imperative impulse. Conflict is inevitable.

The unevenness of the conflict is aggravated by the fact that the male, in addition to possessing superior knowledge, employs dishonourable tactics. This is not a careless accusation, but a statement of fact. Please know that

 *No genuine full-blooded male is trustworthy.*

not even that nice youth next door, or that sweet boy you have just been introduced to, or the fellow you met at the church social. For by some kind of osmosis, they absorb from one another the tenets of a universal code which dictates their low behaviour towards women.* No

 So respected an historian as Carlyle said, "A mystic bond of brotherhood makes all men one."

11

matter how chivalrous, romantic, idealistic, virtuous, honourable, ethical, high-minded and noble he may be— if he is a man, his motives and methods are base.

Clearly, such a creature is dangerous. This fact is recognized in many countries where the customs are older and wiser than ours—where no self-respecting parent will allow his daughter to be alone with a man, with *any* man, no matter how repulsive he may be. It is true that this system is prevalent in warmer climes, but no matter what a man's climate or antecedents may be, his blood is always hot. To be exact, in sun and in shade, winter and summer, as long as he is alive and healthy, man's constant temperature is 98·6° Fahrenheit—a temperature at which, the Weather Bureau advises, eggs can be fried on the pavement.

Frankly, I realize there is little or no chance of introducing the duenna system into the social life of the West. Girls expect freedom and they should have it—within certain limits of decency, of course. (Surely no self-respecting woman would want complete freedom, such as men enjoy.)

But for the degree of freedom she *is* permitted, the female should be carefully prepared. Every effort must be made to equalize the contest between her and the enemy —man. For, in the immortal words of Ovid, "*Militiae species amor est*"—or, "Love is a kind of warfare." And man does his warring on woman with an impudent disregard for the established rules of civilized combat. He will take the fortress or ravish the citadel, only to abandon it and go on to some other mischief. He wants no captive to take home with him. Once the battle is over, he pleasures only in reflecting on, and boasting of, the bodies he has left behind.

In a word, man is a ruthless warrior. Shall we then continue to permit him to come on the battlefield armed to the teeth, tough, experienced, covered by a thick protective armour, with inside information about his victim's defences and a well-laid plan of attack—to confront a trusting, romantic girl who does not even know there is a war on? Is it fair to pit green, untried novices against hardened, trigger-happy troops? No, no, no, no, no! I would send every girl forth with an ironclad defence, a fair estimate of the power and the quality of the enemy, and a thorough knowledge of the strategy he will use. Her education must include a detailed study of the Methods of Intrigue used by man—his motivations, his strengths, and his weaknesses.

It is true, of course, that Experience is the best teacher. Unfortunately, in order to obtain a full and varied experience, a girl would necessarily lose that which she needs the experience in order to protect. Worse, she might lose it in her first skirmish and learn nothing thereby . . . (that is, nothing that would be useful to her in future encounters). It is quite possible that she will lose it over and over again, with unpleasant or embittering

results, before she has acquired enough knowledge to conduct herself intelligently. And then it is somewhat late —she is exhausted by many defeats and scarred by disappointments. Like a nation too often overcome by its foes, she has lost her zest for battle.

To those for whom it is not too late—to the young, the untried, the inexperienced, the curious, the indignant, and the undiscouraged, is this book dedicated.

It would be unwise for anyone to read *The Unfair Sex* in a spirit of idle curiosity, since there is always the danger that words written purely to instruct, to disillusion and to dissuade, may, by some strange alchemy of contact between the writer and the reader's mind, serve to pique, arouse, and incite.

Therefore, if you are a strong little virgin, justifiably smug and secure in your virtue, leave these lessons to your weak and less fortunate sisters. If you are a wife, which naturally precludes any interest in men, put this book aside. It is unbecoming for a married woman to make a study of subjects that smack of the erotic. And if you are a man there is nothing in these pages to interest you, since they contain only that which you already know—an analysis of your motivations and an exposé of your methods in the plundering, despoiling, and fleecing of the gentler sex.

I address myself to those unmarried females who lay no claim to chastity—and those, still pure, who fear for their virginity. It is my intention to supply you with the kind of factual knowledge which is the only substitute for experience; to give you the benefit of data gathered by one who, in her tireless search for the truth about men, has earned the title, "Woman of the World."* Armed with the information contained in these pages, you will be qualified to take on any man; you will be acquainted with

 A Woman of the World is one who has eaten well of the apple and wears the core like a crown.

the hazards, the traps, and the pleasures to be expected; and you will be apprised of the practical disadvantages of giving yourself without first obtaining a lifetime guarantee of service.

A book of this kind is ill-adapted to controversial subjects, and I have therefore omitted all reference to

## LOVE

the very definition of which is open to endless dispute. On only one point is there universal agreement: The girl who is in love, or thinks she is in love, is beyond the reach of reason. She who is sincerely interested in her own well-being will avoid that emotional aberration as she would the black plague.

If some of the statements contained herein seem illogical, or if one chapter appears to contradict another, remember that the author is a member of that sex which is notorious for its inconsistencies. Moreover, Life itself is full of contradictions. Ask yourself not, Is it logical?—but, Is it true?

## CHAPTER TWO

# False Prophets and
# Propaganda

BEFORE PROCEEDING with these studies, it is necessary to clear away a number of traditional misconceptions which tend to operate against your best interests.

Let us begin with the generally accepted theory that "Mother knows best." If you brush aside the sentimental halo that surrounds motherhood and examine this claim dispassionately, you must realize that it is not entirely true. The fact that a woman has achieved marriage and borne children does not automatically qualify her as an authority on men.

My own mother contented herself with mumbling some vague and embarrassed warnings, which I interpreted to mean that I would promptly have a baby if I let a boy kiss my lips. (It was not until almost a year later that I received further information on this subject from a more reliable source—the little boy next door.)

Of course, that was a generation ago—but today's

children do not fare much better. These are the precepts currently in vogue:

... Men have no use for a girl who is promiscuous.

... You have a mind of your own. If anything happens it's your own fault.

... Any intelligent girl knows how to handle herself with men.

... Just behave like a lady, and you'll have nothing to worry about.

... If you don't behave yourself, you'll never get a husband.

... I'm not concerned about you, dear. The apple never falls far from the tree.

Is there a thimbleful of truth in these dogmatic pronouncements? Do they gibe with reality? Not at all. Promiscuity does not lead to loneliness, few females have minds of their own, the brilliant ones usually handle their love affairs like idiots, men are not discouraged by either good or bad manners, and girls are not apples. From these examples you may judge how poor is mother's "best."

Not only do these well-meaning ladies give false counsel, they also create a set of false standards, leading their daughters to expect a popularity which few can attain, and a chivalry that does not exist. Have you ever heard a mother reminisce about all the dances she was *not* invited to, all the Saturday nights she was dateless, all the boys she never heard from again? OR—about the dangerous encounters and narrow escapes she had? I doubt it. Every daughter's mother gives the impression that the pre-marital years are one big whirl of carefree gaiety, with a bountiful supply of dates and proposals.

She does this not because she wants to deceive, but because time and the female ego have helped her to forget the difficulties of those years when it was incumbent on her to attract the fugitive male even as she evaded his artful snares.

It is too bad daughters cannot rely on their mothers for honest information. For when mama's never-never land fails to materialize, a girl's disappointment is often so acute as to render her overanxious, indiscriminate, and otherwise unfit for battle.

Mothers are not the only false prophets. I put them first as a mark of respect, and also because their influence is so great. Just as much harm is done by the psychologists, doctors, educators, and free-lance writers who compose popular articles for reputable magazines. These authorities either bemoan or condone the fact that our moral code is changing, that few girls are virgins when they reach the altar, that more and more women are acceding to the demands made on them by men.

It is a grave mistake to publish this information. When women read that their competitors are giving something away, they feel obliged to do likewise, and when men read of the courtesies extended to their brothers, they naturally expect the same for themselves. Thus this vicious propaganda depreciates and reduces to the commonplace that which should be constantly advertised as precious, prized, and difficult to attain.

It is not sensible to allow one's greatest asset to be belittled. We must combat this adverse publicity. And it can be combated, because—fortunately—there are no reliable statistics to support it. Protest, therefore, against such damaging articles, deny and ridicule them wherever two or more are gathered, boycott the periodicals that print them, and encourage the dissemination of facts and legends which will enhance the position of womankind— for mighty is the power of the printed word.

Other forms of propaganda are equally potent. There is in existence a whole collection of slogans, songs, and superstitions, which by virtue of constant repetition have come to be accepted as fact.

A common example is that little catch phrase, "Feminine Intuition." This implies that every female possesses an uncanny power which guides her in making correct decisions. Logic, reason, or some knowledge of the subject in question are deemed superfluous—for a woman's sixth sense cannot lead her wrong . . . they say.

There is no such thing as Feminine Intuition. It is a masculine invention designed to make you feel there is no need to use what sense you do have.

The "Wisdom of Eve" is another fantasy, somewhat similar to intuition. It is intended to make women believe they have an inborn and comprehensive understanding of man, and are, from childhood on, complete mistresses of the art of coquetry.

This is too absurd to merit discussion. Women simply blunder their way through until they reach the haven of marriage. The Wisdom of Eve, indeed! Everyone knows how foolish *that* lady was.

THE UNFAIR SEX

"Be good, sweet maid, and let who will be clever."
There is an obvious contradiction in this little gem. A
maid who is not clever is unlikely to remain good.

"Woman is like a flower." We are told that Man is like
a honey-bee hopping from flower to flower, and that
Woman is like a flower with honey for *Just one bee*. What
Flower closes her petals to What Bee? We are more discriminating than any flower and should consider such a
simile an insult.

"To love is better than to be loved." This is like saying
it is better to be the horse than the driver.

"Wrap him around your little finger" insinuates that
a maid can do as she wills with a man. A great many girls
proceed blithely under the assumption that this is true,
and are very much surprised when they are the ones who
get wrapped.

There are, of course, many many more untruths in
circulation. Examine, test, analyse all words and phrases
before you place your faith in them. Too often is
dangerous propaganda hidden away in a little old cliché.

## CHAPTER THREE

# Why a Man Wants
# What He Wants

*"Every man is as God made him, ay, and often worse."* .
—CERVANTES

WHAT causes an otherwise upright member of society to lie, scheme, cheat, and trick his way into a woman's confidence? What drives him to plunder the sex which he himself labels the weaker one? What motivates a man? With no attempt to pretty-up the picture, or soften what may be a blow to feminine self-esteem I list here, in order of their importance...

23

*The Sixteen Joys of Man*

## 1.

### *Joy of Ownership*

A man needs the comfort and the convenience of a possession. Like his car, it may not be exactly the model he prefers, but it will take him where he wants to go. In this respect, there is a cozy feeling of luxury in having two, or even three.

2.

*Joy of Revenge*

Subjugated by Woman in his childhood and later en-
slaved by her in marriage, he revels in the opportunity to
humble her by the only means open to him.

### 3.

*Joy of Conquest*

Man finds gratification in besting an opponent, whether at golf or tennis or whatnot. He plays hard to win—not the girl, but the trophy.

## 4.

*Joy of Verification*

In a world filled with doubts and confusion, many a man feels the need of continually proving to himself that he is an authentic male.

**5.**

*Joy of Bragging*

A goodly portion of a man's satisfaction is derived from the telling of his victories to other men—and basking in the admiration he earns thereby.

**6.**

*Joy of Trespassing*

The contrariness of Man's nature impels him to walk where the sign says "Keep Off," and to enter doors marked "No Admittance."

30

### 7.

*Joy of Identification with the Herd*

No man wants to be different from other men. He pursues women as a matter of good form. It is manly, it is *comme il faut*, and it makes him "one of the boys."

**8.**

*Joy of Stoking the Ego*

As in being elected House Captain, or gaining admission to an exclusive club, the acquisition of a desirable woman gives a man's ego an enormous lift.

## 9.

### *Joy of Stealing*

There is a very special and acute pleasure in stealing a woman from a friend or an enemy. It satisfies a primitive masculine urge.

## 10.

### *Joy of Nature*

This is the simple delight of fulfilling Nature's demands.

34

## 11.

### *Joy of Getting Something for Nothing*

Spendthrift or miser, no man can resist the pleasure of getting something for nothing.

## 12.

### *Joy of Compensation*

A man whom success has eluded in other fields finds comfort in his victories over women.

36

13.

*Joy of Escape*

Man finds Woman the most soothing of all opiates. In her arms he can forget all his worries and his woes.

## 14.

### *Joy of Exploration*

It is fun to undo the wrappings and ribbons of a carefully done-up package and explore the contents. Each new package seems to hold the promise of some unexpected surprise.

## 15.

### *Joy of Destruction*

A proud or inaccessible girl fills the male with an inexplicable desire to "knock her off her high horse," to see her with her hair disarranged, her make-up blurred, and her poise shattered.

## 16.

*Joy of Performance*

Any sort of ability, native or acquired, fills a man with pride and the desire to exercise his skill.

# WHY A MAN WANTS WHAT HE WANTS

Be realistic. Each time you are tempted, ask yourself—"Why does he want me?" An honest answer will remind you of the unflattering reasons. Realize it is not an honour to be asked. Many girls regard it as a compliment or a declaration of love, and find out too late how mistaken they are. It is quite possible he does not even like you. Man is notoriously undiscriminating, demanding no more of his partner than that she be a female. His selection of you as that partner is based not on your irresistibility, but on your availability.

Naturally, Man is cunning enough to realize that if you know the kind of reasons he has for wanting you, his chances for success will be slight. But he does not trouble himself to invent a nice motive with which to deceive you; he ignores the whole subject and trusts to luck that you will do the same. Do not disappoint him in this respect. For it is both gauche and unfeminine to reveal the fact that your mental processes are at work. To embarrass a man is not desirable. What is important is that you outwit him.

Men know full well that their attitude is a detestable one, and in an attempt to justify themselves, they resort to a number of

 *Petty accusations against women*

They claim that:

A. Women are Underhand—they offer friendship, admiration, and affection as a bait to trick men into matrimony against their will.

B. Women are Insincere—they pretend to like a man for himself, when actually they are interested in the entertainment he can provide.

C. Women are Shallow—they seek to annex men merely to satisfy their own vanity, and to show off in front of other women.

With these hypothetical feminine objectives in mind, Man plans his Offensive and Defensive measures as follows:

AGAINST MARRIAGE

Shortly after adolescence sets in, every male becomes convinced that all women are out to "get him." If a woman so much as smile at him, be she beautiful, talented, rich, or in truth too good for him in every respect, he will immediately suspect she wants to marry him.

In reality, Man, being the clever beast he is, rarely is caught unless he wants to be. Fortunately, a moment comes in the life of almost every man when the comforts of marriage seem to outweigh the joys of freedom, and that is when he submits to "capture." But, fearful that some crafty female will catch him before he is ready, he faces each girl he meets with the thought, "She'll get me if I don't get her first." The point I ask you to observe here is not that man is Ruthless and Vengeful, but that

  *Man is always on guard*

No matter how guileless or stupid he may appear, he is *always on guard:*

AGAINST EXPLOITATION

The bargaining Man does in connection with entertainment is on a very petty scale. There is one type—

fortunately a minority group—known as Free-Loader. He makes it a rule to give nothing—to spend not one penny. His credo is: Keep what you've got, take what you can get, and always ask for more. But the average man is not guilty of such pinch-penny methods. Rather he is like a sharp little tradesman, trying to get as much as he can in exchange for a minimum expenditure of time and money. Carefully he rations out the pleasures he gives. So many dinners, so many theatre tickets, so many bottles of Scotch weighed against the amount of progress he is making towards his goal. He is prompted not by stinginess, but by the determination that no woman shall make a profit on him.

# THE UNFAIR SEX

## AGAINST ANNEXATION

Men enjoy the rather smug belief that women cannot get along without them. And they are right. Man is of extreme importance to Women. Indeed, no woman should be without one. There are places she cannot enter without an escort, either by edict of law or social precedent, but even for the most ordinary occasions, nothing makes a woman feel more chic, no accessory sets her off to better advantage, than a presentable man.

There is also the matter of prestige. A woman who goes about without an escort loses face with men, with other women, with herself, and, what is more painful, with her own family.

This feminine dependence, this need, man employs as a weapon. If his desires are not met on demand, he gives the lady to understand that she will no longer have the use of his services. Since there is no pressure the female can bring to bear, and since there is no substitute for a man, she is in a rather helpless position. For stronger than all temptation, more persuasive than any argument, is the fear that he will go elsewhere if he does not have his way.

Fortunately, in the feminine make-up there is a strength, spiked with a soupcon of shrewdness, which enables a decent percentage of our sex to stand up to the threat of masculine non-participation and defy it, taking the consequences if necessary. Were this not so, we would be completely at the mercy of the whims and wishes of the male.

It is deplorable that the weaker woman, with a selfish disregard for the consequences to our sex as a whole, accepts the unreasonable terms foisted on us by Man.

If this practice became widespread, men would soon deem it unnecessary to surrender in marriage at all. And without marriage, *there is no divorce*.

*Remember the alimony!*

It is my dream, and not a hopeless one, that someday our sex will unite, that we will present an undivided, impregnable front to all males and force them to discontinue their unfair practices. Until that day, each of you must fight as best you can your individual battles. Remember always the Sixteen Joys that motivate the enemy—and do not permit yourself to forget them in the heat of the fray.

## CHAPTER FOUR

# And What He Does
# To Get It

NATURALLY, the methods used by Man through the ages have varied with the manners and mores of the period to which he was born. At this moment in history, the methods employed are fairly simple, and any female of less than average intelligence can, with a little careful study, become thoroughly familiar with them.

As an example of how methods change with the times, I ask that you call to mind the False Promise of Marriage which in grandma's day was so effective in causing the downfall of innocent girls. Except for an isolated case which may, from time to time, crop up in the hinterlands, this is now obsolete.

In mother's time, the popular twist was Free Love. If a man said "I love you," he could easily convince a girl that further benediction was unnecessary and an insult to Havelock Ellis.

An interesting development took place a decade later, during The Great Depression, when an impoverished people was obliged to seek simple, inexpensive pleasures. With typical native hardiness and good humour, Man evolved a philosophy which characterized the spirit of the time, and was expressed in the popular song "The Best Things in Life Are Free." Women were stampeded by such reasoning and fell right and left, astonished victims of the *Zeitgeist*.

At present, Man's method of attack is based on four closely inter-related principles: Flattery, Conversation Piece, Intrigue, and The Mating Instinct. These are the foundation stones of seduction.

## 1. FLATTERY

The female has a pitiful weakness for flattery, and men, with their usual lack of good sportsmanship, prey on

this weakness. It is difficult for a woman to dislike or distrust someone who admires her, and no compliment is too absurd for her credence. Sometimes her feeble intuitive powers cause a stirring of doubt. This she quickly smothers with such sensible questions as, "Why would he say it if he didn't think so?"—or, "What can he gain by lying to me?"

To those who have wilfully deluded themselves with such queries, I reply:—Man is the kind of hunter who would make a little bird dizzy with chloroform before aiming his rifle. Even a stripling knows that women are rendered weak and defenceless by "sweet talk."

There are, of course, other forms of flattery—frequent phone calls, love letters, expensive entertainment, steady dating, and gifts. But whatever form a man's flattery may take, and even if it is sincere (as sometimes happens) it is used with a complete awareness of the effect it will have on you, and with a resolute purpose in mind.

Keep your wits about you. Certainly bask in the man's adulation and enjoy his attentions. But remember, flattery is like strong drink—it can befuddle your brain, warp your judgment, and literally knock you off your feet. Do not permit this to happen to you.

## 2. CONVERSATION PIECE

"To speak of love is to make love."* In a rather close approximation of this theory, men invariably channel the conversation into a discussion of the male-female relationship. This is not only a topic that everyone finds fascinating—it is virtually inexhaustible and calculated to stimulate improper thoughts. It is unlike that other favourite, the weather, in that people who talk about sex are apt to end up doing something about it. One might think it a simple matter to avoid this danger area of conversation. But man has a nimble tongue. He does not

 Balzac.

always embark openly on a discussion of the theme dearest to his heart. Instead he leads you into it obliquely by introducing apparently harmless subjects, such as a case of rape in the current news, the mating cry of the Siamese cat, hygiene as taught in the schools, or the interesting case-history of a nymphomaniac he once knew. His manner is matter-of-fact as he conducts you through an

academic and then a personal discussion on mores and morals, tackling the most delicate subjects with aplomb. No physiological, no personal idiosyncrasy escapes utterance or dissection, and by the time you have had three dates, you are on a far more intimate footing with him than most women ever achieve with their husbands. This

49

is terribly dangerous. The atmosphere becomes heavy with words and thoughts, and even in retrospect a girl can rarely remember the point at which she became tangled in the lush undergrowth of the verbiage.

Do not underestimate the potency of the spoken word. We must guard our ears as carefully as other parts of our persons and keep our conversation as innocent as our actions. From verbal to physical intimacy is a very small step.

## 3. INTRIGUE

I use this term to describe the strategy employed by a man in persuading a woman to give herself to him. Intrigue may take the form of a Line, a Device, or a Technique—or any combination of these three. The Line is a verbal assault, and generally comes into play after the subject has been softened by Flattery, but sometimes the two are worked in together and so skilfully blended that it is almost impossible to discern where one starts and the other leaves off. In such a case, a girl may find herself saying, "Oh, thank you," instead of "Oh!! Stop it!"

To ensure success, some men resort to the Device—a trick of accessory or locale.

Those who use a Technique rely on a studied course of action to produce the desired reactions and emotions in the female.

The amount of effort a man puts forth and the lengths to which he will carry his Intrigue depend upon the resistance he encounters and the desirability of the woman in question. *Every* Line, Device and Technique, without exception, depends to some extent on—

## 4. THE MATING INSTINCT

It is a recognized fact that females as well as males are subject to the Mating Instinct. Instinct is an unreasoning force, capable of leading one into folly and even self-destruction. Witness the poor lemming who, at Nature's bidding, rushes headlong into the sea to drown.

For their own protection, girls are taught to thwart their Mating Instinct until the conventionally approved moment arrives. But in spite of this, it remains an unknowable quantity and, like a wild beast held captive, may slip its bonds at any moment.

Do not fall into a careless attitude of self-confidence in the foolish belief that you have no Mating Instinct, or that if you have, yours is under perfect control. As resolutely as you defend yourself from Man, you must defend yourself from the enemy within.

All males know the unpredictable character of the feminine libido. Their Intrigues are designed to encourage and incite it, to furnish the female with an alibi for succumbing to it, and to undermine the safeguards she has built to restrain it.

* * *

In summation, Man faces Woman with a thorough understanding of her weaknesses, a cynical estimate of her designs on him, and a purposeful plan of attack.

## CHAPTER FIVE

# Lines

*"That man that hath a tongue, I say, is no man,*
*If with his tongue he cannot win a woman."*
—SHAKESPEARE

THERE are in existence so many types of lines, and such countless variations of each type, that it is impossible to compile a comprehensive catalogue in a work of this size. However, you will find here blueprints of the most widely used lines, and if you have a thorough understanding of these, you should be able to recognize and classify the variations when you come across them.

## LINE NUMBER ONE

### Don't Be a Kid

This is used exclusively on virgins—especially very young ones. A girl in her teens cannot bear to be told that she is hardly more than a child, and the sting of this accusation can drive her to commit foolish acts of bravado.

Following is a little dramatic sketch which illustrates

the pattern a man follows in undermining such a girl's morale, and laughing away her scruples:

SCENE: A park bench, a sofa, or a car,
TIME: Night or day.

He: Why not?

She: Because.

He: That's no reason. Give me a good adult reason.

She: Well—it's not right.

He: Who says so? Your mother? When are you going to grow up and start thinking for yourself?

She: Well, *I* don't think it's right. Nice girls don't do those things.

He: Where did you hear that? Isn't Sally a nice girl? And June? And your sister Isobel?

She: Of course they are, and don't try to tell me *they*—

He: Sure. Do you think everyone's as childish as you?

She: (shocked and indignant) Well, I don't believe my sister would—

He: Okay, okay. Have it your way. But everyone says you're a—

She: I'm a what?

He: Never mind.

She: You tell me this minute.

He: (putting his arm round her) Well, all right, but remember—you asked for it.

She: Go ahead.

He: Well, everyone thinks you're a kid. (Shocked and insulted, she gasps.) Look, honey—I think the world of you, but you really are a—awfully immature.

She: I don't think it's immature to have morals.

He: *Sure* you should have morals. You shouldn't cheat— or steal. But how can you hurt anyone just by growing up? You're missing all the fun. Everybody does what they please, except you. I mean it—you're the *only* one.

She: (weakening) I'm sure I'm not the *only* one.

**He:** (laughing) Nobody pays attention to those old-fashioned ideas any more. It's a little peculiar for a girl your age to be a virgin (he kisses her gently). Naturally, I wouldn't want you to be promiscuous. But with someone you *know*, and who likes you a helluva lot—that's different.

**She:** (to herself, as tears come to her eyes) Is it true? Am I the only one? Are they all laughing at me? Is that why I didn't get asked to the Robinsons' house party? Does everyone think I'm just a kid?

**He:** Maybe I shouldn't have said anything. Maybe I'd better leave you alone, and come back a year from now. Drop me a postcard when you're all grown up. (He kisses her tenderly.) After all, you are only a kid.

**She:** Stop saying that!

**He:** (with an amused smile) Well, you're not a real woman.

**She:** (resolutely) Oh, yes I am.

**He:** (solemnly) Are you?

**She:** Yes. Yes!

### CURTAINS

Too often our little girl takes the plunge, determined to prove to herself and the world that she is not a kid.

## LINE NUMBER TWO

### *What Are You Saving It For?*

This is a psychological attack designed to frighten any girl over twenty-one. By insinuation and implication, it plants enfeebling thoughts in your head, such as:

I'm not so young any more.

In ten years I'll have faded and no one will want me. Maybe no one will ever ask me again.

I'm a coward.

I'll spend my old age regretting the lost opportunities of my youth.

The sins of omission are greater than those of commission.

There are, of course, some advantages to having an open mind, but here is evidence of the dangerous kind of claptrap that can be tossed in if you are not careful.

Having thrown you into a state of apprehension, the despicable cad proceeds to offer you spurious reasons for letting him have his way.

He points out that yours is a foolish economy: why put aside for your old age that for which you will have no need in your old age? He preaches that sharing brings greater happiness than hoarding. That you can never make up for lost time. That it is unwise to put off for tomorrow what can be done today. That—well, there is no end to his sophistries.

This is not the kind of Line which will precipitate a girl into a man's arms, but it does send her to bed brooding. As often as not, after a few nights of reflection, she sees the logic in all this false reasoning and decides to throw away the savings of a lifetime.

The one amusing feature here is that occasionally the man who advances this Line is by-passed, and the fruits of his efforts are enjoyed by someone the girl likes better.

# THE UNFAIR SEX

## Sex Is Beautiful

A man who has a good vocabulary and no conscience can easily pervert your sense of values. With high-flown words and verbal sleight-of-hand he manages to make sex seem beautiful and continence unaesthetic. His tones are lyrical as he rhapsodizes on the wonders of nature, the glories of the human body and the ineffable loveliness of carnal desire.

Loftily he declares he cannot respect a girl who feels that any wrong attaches to that which he deems pure and splendid, and which in fact was a sacrament in ancient, more golden civilizations. *Honi soit qui mal y pense* is his motto\*—which puts you at a distinct disadvantage, for everything you say in rebuttal is bound to sound indelicate. You are made to feel so embarrassed for your gaucherie that to save face you hasten to assure him you, too, think it is positively beautiful. You are obliged to agree that the union of two people is the highest possible expression of human fulfilment; that in this way, one may put oneself in harmony with the universe, and pulsate in rhythm with the music of the spheres. You swim together in a sea of rhetoric—and end up under the old apple tree.

If you do, do not expect him to linger long. His kind is like the humming-bird, sipping loveliness and joy from many flowers—because it is all so unbearably beautiful.

LINE NUMBER FOUR

## The Rush

Leaning heavily on the basic principle of Flattery, the man who gives you The Rush dedicates himself to the task of inflating your ego. And how pleasant this is for the ego.

 "Shamed be he who thinks evil of it."

What a glow it gives you to be deluged with phone calls, dates, compliments, gifts—to hear him say he Never knew anyone like you, you are Disrupting his life, he Can't put you out of his mind, and similar warmed-up cabbage.

I knew a man who disciplined himself strictly while engaged in giving a Rush. He sent flowers twice a week, wrote love letters every day, and disturbed me regularly in the middle of the night with a phone call. He explained this last display of devotion by saying he could not sleep for thinking of me—that he had to hear the sound of my voice or go mad. You can imagine how much this particular attention impressed me. Actually, as I later discovered, he always slept soundly, and had used an alarm clock to wake him at three every morning for the sole purpose of pleasing me.

This is one small sample of the lengths to which a man will go in carrying out a successful Rush. And what girl can resist that sort of thing? It's the kind of romantic delight you start searching for in your teens, the high fantastical gallantry that is dear to the female heart.

A man sometimes telescopes the Rush, and gives you a rushed Rush. He catches your attention with an incendiary gaze compounded in equal parts of pleasure, amazement, and admiration—and three minutes after you have met, he is kissing your hand and showering you with the most devastating compliments. He forces you to admit that something happened to you, too, the instant you saw each other—that a kind of electricity crackled in the air when your eyes first met his.

So intense is his ardour that if you are at all combustible you catch fire from him. You have the uncanny feeling that this has all happened before—perhaps in some other incarnation (or maybe you saw it in a movie). By the time your romance is one hour old, he has told you all his ambitions and plans. You, of course, are the Girl of His Dreams, and before you know what you are doing, you are off in a secluded nook making his dreams come true. There is no time to think. You are limp. You feel faint. You see pin-wheels in front of your eyes. This, he tells you, is something rare and inflammable and uncontrollable—this is a flash fire.*

Rush or rushed Rush, even with fair warning and all the signals plainly marked, you will never admit that you are being fed a Line, preferring to indulge yourself in the luxury of such adulation.

You will allow yourself to be adored, wooed, flattered, pursued, wined, dined, and Valentined, and literally Rushed off your feet.

LINE NUMBER FIVE

## The Charity Drive

*"Beggars mounted run their horse to death."*—SHAKESPEARE

In Number Five a man appeals to your good nature with his bad one. Though effective enough to stand by itself, the Drive is also utilized as a bolstering measure at the tag-end of another Line.

It is usually sprung at the teeter-totter moment known as "Now or Never." This is the moment when it comes to a girl that she has gone too far, and a little flash of intuition warns her that if she does not stop now—instantly—she will not stop at all—ever. It is then that a man starts plugging away with his Charity Drive.

He pleads, he cajoles, he begs, he urges and coaxes, he wheedles and implores you to be kind to him. He becomes a miserable, frantic creature, too weak to control his desire (though his arms seem amazingly strong). Stealthily he creeps into your heart with his piteous murmurings:—

 More likely it is a flash in the pan.

"... please ... only ... just ... I promise ... please ... ah, please, please ... oh, you're so wonderful ... please..." And sometimes the most craven of these beggars will actually say, "Be good to me."

What manner of woman can withstand the heart-rending pleas of a wretched fellow being who grovels thus at her feet? Would you turn away a tramp who asked in like fashion for a meal or a bed to sleep in? And this is no tramp, but a nice young man whose kisses you have enjoyed. He is humbling himself. He kneels before you, stripped (so to speak)—divested of all pretence and all dignity. How can you deny him what he wants? Alas, you cannot. For women are notoriously tender-hearted, and most Charity Drives are all too successful.

It is a continual source of amazement to those who make contributions, that once appeased, the pathetic little beggar loses his humility. He becomes a happy full-blooded male, master of himself and of the situation. Unmindful of the kindness which put him where he is, he feels no gratitude towards his benefactor. And, as if he has received nothing more than his honest due, he goes on his carefree way, seeking alms at other doors.

So take heed, all you overemotional, oversentimental girls, and restrain yourselves from giving every time a cup is rattled under your noses. Remember, there are organizations to take care of the needy.

LINE NUMBER SIX

*Sneak Preview*

SCENE: A sofa, the back seat of a car, a hammock, or any place where two people can sit together cosily.

He: (His arm is around her. She likes him and he knows it.) Nine-tenths of all divorces are caused by incompatibility.

She: Tsk!

He: I'm not taking any risk of that when I get married.

She: No?

He: Oh, no! I don't believe in going into things blindly.

She: No.

He: Take us for instance.

She: Yes?

He: Well, as far as I know, you're a wonderful girl. You suit me fine. I'd be proud to have my children call a girl like you Mother.

She: Oh, darling—do you mean—(he interrupts her with a kiss).

He: Only we'd be crazy to think about marriage. We don't even know if we're compatible.

She: Oh.

He: After all, marriage is a sacred thing.

She: I know!

He: Do you think it should be entered into lightly?

She: Oh, no! But after all, sex isn't the most important thing about it. If two people—

He: Listen—you're talking like a child. Sure it isn't the most important thing to us *consciously*, but to our glands and our brain-cells and our chemical reactions and stuff, it's everything. We can't control them—they control *us*. If they aren't satisfied, they can put your whole marriage on the rocks. And what'll people call it? Incompatability!

She: But—what if we do—uh—the sensible thing, and we find out we—we're incompatible? Then where will I be?

He: You'll be a hundred times better off than if you married the wrong man, won't you?

She: I suppose. But do you mean that if you and I do—uh—that if we are—uh—that we'd get married?

He: Listen—we have no right even to think about marriage at this point. We don't know each other well enough. Two people have to *really know* each other before they—(he kisses her). Don't you agree?

She: Well—

He: Don't you?

She: Yes, but—(he interrupts her with kisses).

He: You sweet little darling (he kisses her frantically).


Foolish, wasn't she?

Do you intend to tell all before you get married? That your uncle was imprisoned for making a book? That your hands swell if you wash dishes? Or that you once were jilted? Not unless you are a very silly girl! For he is hiding many bits of vital information from you. Only after you are married will you discover that he picks his teeth—that he doesn't believe in bathing every day—that he sleeps with all windows wide open even in zero weather—or that his mother is going to live with you.

Why, then, take the risk of supplying him with a concrete reason for not marrying you? Suppose you were agreeable enough to take this test with three or four prospective bridegrooms in turn, and failed each time. Is it not better to be incompatibly married than never to be married at all?

# THE UNFAIR SEX

Marrying is, at best, like buying a pig in a poke. This has always been so, and there is no reason to effect a change now. The civilized male of today should be grateful·for the privilege of viewing the legs of his prospective bride. There was a time, and not so very long ago, when he was forced to be content with seeing little more than her face before arriving at the point where it was too late for him to turn back. Man is truly becoming spoiled when he demands detailed and intimate proof of your every qualification.

I say—don't give it to him!

## LINE NUMBER SEVEN

### *Where Does It Hurt?*

Like a St. Bernard dog, Number Seven comes to succour you, bearing a keg of solace and comforts. It is his mission to restore you to happiness after a great sorrow.

Have you quarrelled with your mother? Or muffed an exam? Or lost your job? Or your wrist-watch? Has some man hurt you?* Whatever your trouble may be, whatever your hurt—this dog will kiss it and make it better.

He listens patiently and attentively as you recite your troubles, and his little gestures of affection seem so well-meant you accept them gratefully. In an indifferent world, here is a human being filled with sympathy and warmth, someone who is only too eager to take you in his arms and make you feel adorable, precious and wanted.

While he keeps your mind fixed on your sorrows, he advances his own cause. He strokes you with strong, comforting hands. He is your friend. He encourages you to cry, knowing that tears render a woman soft and resistless. Slowly, sneakily, he encroaches on your preserves, pushing

 Very often he does not trust to luck, but himself inflicts the necessary wound.

back your boundaries bit by bit, until by the Law of Gradual Envelopment he has taken everything.

Conversely, a man may seek instead of offer sympathy. Perhaps his wife has left him, or he has a tooth-ache, or he has wrecked his new car. If sad movies bring tears to your eyes, if a homeless kitten causes a choking sensation in your throat, if you have a trace of womanly compassion in your make-up—you cannot help but hold out your arms to such a man and offer comfort.

Once in your arms, any man—no matter how poignant his grief—is able to think of but one thing.

And you—you are softened by pity and brimming over with the milk of human kindness. How good you are, how understanding. How dear is the pleasure that comes of helping a fellow creature.

Yours is the comforting bosom, yours the sympathetic embrace, yours the bottomless well of goodness. Ah, me. Down, down you go, waving the banner of an Angel of Mercy.

LINE NUMBER EIGHT

*The Bedside Manner*

In gentle murmuring tones, the man with the Bedside Manner misleads, deceives, beguiles and betrays you, giving false comfort as he gets on with his work, like a dentist calming a nervous patient.

First he inspires you with confidence and trust, then he manoeuvres you into a position that makes it easy for him to operate and difficult for you to get away. Softly, kindly, he whispers, ". . . all right . . . it's all right . . . don't be afraid . . . I just want to be close to you . . . like this . . . no harm in that, is there? . . . relax . . . relax . . . I wouldn't do anything to hurt you . . . don't you trust me? . . . well, then, relax . . . there we are . . . that's my girl . . . I'm not going to do anything you don't want me to do . . ."

Lulled by the anaesthetic effect of his words, you relax, relax, relax. When you come to, you discover with a shock that you've lost your tooth or whatever.

## Line Number Nine

### *Supersalesman*

The man who achieves success with Number Nine is invariably a master of several Lines, and moderately conversant with all. He does not hesitate to bring a group of them into play against the same girl—tossing them together like a green salad. Whereas you might recognize a Line if it were delivered singly, in orthodox fashion, you are sure to be confused by the mixture he serves you.

His routine is similar to that used by men who sell encyclopaedias and vacuum-cleaners from door to door. And he applies their method of "passing the order-book early and often." He deliberately presents you with the idea of buying, long before he has warmed you up to that point. Then he calmly accepts your shocked refusal and starts over again, to retreat and attack, retreat and attack, until eventually the sight of the order blank no longer frightens you. You become accustomed to it, your vigilance relaxes; it has a harmless, familiar look.

Each time you meet, Supersalesman picks up where he left off, or starts a fresh approach. He badgers you, argues with you, reasons and pleads with you, and though your resolve be hard as stone, it will be worn away by the relentless dripping of his words. You begin to accept the salesman's conviction that some day you will buy. From this to "Eventually, why not now?" is a small jump. And suddenly you find you have bought yourself something you did not know you wanted.

LINE NUMBER TEN

### The Scientific Approach

Modern woman, perhaps because she lives in an age that glorifies Science, has a tendency to spurn the tried and true principles which served her grandmothers so well. She foolishly reasons that if a course of action is scientific it must be good. It is the clear-thinking, logical female who is most apt to be taken in by the Scientific Approach. But even the less intelligent are swayed by the music of a convincing male voice as it expounds this specious theory.

If you offer the usual old-fashioned arguments such as— "I'm afraid," or "I'm saving myself for a husband," he smiles patiently and in a friendly tone starts talking about birds and bees. Gradually, he works his way round to mammals and higher branches of the animal world and concludes by proving that humans, too, are governed by the basic laws of Biology.

You then will be gently coaxed into confessing that you are normal. (If you baulk at this, you are a rarity indeed.)

Very well. If you are normal, you have the same needs as other creatures, have you not? And there he has you! You have been induced to admit that you—the individual, wonderful you, with all your fine airs and dainty habits—are nothing more than a biological pawn, subject to a well-known pattern of wants and needs. This gives you a curiously naked feeling. Pressing his advantage, he declares that when you say "no" you are inhibiting yourself, and with this statement he pivots from Biology into Popular Psychology.

He flings at you such terms as complexes, phobias, inhibitions, neuroses, repressions, suppressions, and frustrations—particularly frustrations. There is a word to strike terror in your heart!

Are you dissatisfied with your job, or your clothes, or your home, or your parents, or yourself? All due to Frustration!

Do you have headaches, or moods of depression, or vague longings for you-know-not-what? Frustration!

Do you read a lot? Frustration!

Do you love the movies? Frustration!

Do you crave affection? Frustration!

Do you have a sense of incompleteness? A feeling of inferiority? Do you wonder what life is all about? Are you overweight? Are you underweight? Frustration! Frustration! FRUSTRATION!!

Accede to the immutable laws of Nature, he states, and you will immediately become happy, popular, and at peace with the world.

If you cannot be persuaded that you are frustrated, you can be intimidated in other ways. He may suggest you have a father-fixation—a sister-, brother-, or mother-fixation. You have a guilt complex. You are immature. You have an unhealthy attitude towards life. And so on and on. There is no end to the physiological, sociological, diabolical arguments he will advance.

Heed him not! What happiness can you expect from a man who puts sex on a prosaic scientific basis? What warmth, affection, or gratitude will be forthcoming from one who wants you to believe you are not giving him a precious gift, but giving yourself a beneficial treatment? Where is the sweet dream of love, the careless rapture, the delicious ecstasy, the feeling of obligation he should have? Where is romance? Certainly not in a test tube.

## LINE NUMBER ELEVEN

### *The Intellectual Approach*

Nothing is ever quite so upsetting to a woman as an appeal to her intellect. Due to a steady stream of male propaganda ridiculing the female mentality, many a woman has come to regard her head as her weakest point. Naturally, this puts her on the defensive, and she will do any number of foolish things in order to seem intelligent.

From the time of the first date, the man who uses the Intellectual Approach impresses his vis-à-vis with the respect he has for her mind. Thus with one and the same stroke he flatters her inordinately, and puts her under obligation to prove, at no matter what cost, that his estimate of her is correct.

By agreeing with him on all major issues, she knows she can retain his respect, and by disagreeing on a few minor

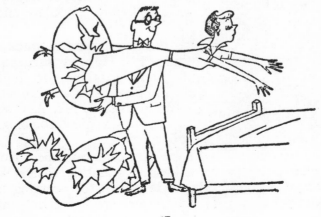

points she hopes to make him think she has a mind of her own. On this cordial basis they have lofty debates on existentatialism, pointillism, chauvinism, hedonism, and nepotism. And, like a boy training a dog, he never fails to reward her with a compliment each time she jumps through a mental hoop.

Made giddy by the altitudes of abstract discussion, flustered by his continual praises, she mechanically echoes his every word, oblivious of where he is leading her. Suddenly she finds herself agreeing as he scoffs at the conventions, the taboos, the restrictions that strive to strangle the Man-Woman relationship.

"Are we children?" he asks. "Are we to be dictated to by a hypocritical society? Must we bow to a set of outmoded rules? Do we need a scrap of paper* to permit us to live as nature intended?"

Before she can adjust her thoughts to the turn the conversation has taken, he rushes onward. "Those rules are all right for the great mass of unthinking people, for the petty bourgeoisie, the puppets who can't reason for themselves. But for people like you and me—it's sheer nonsense."

Fearful of being recognized as a member of that unthinking mass, she quickly joins his more exclusive team. She is no petty bourgeoise, no, no. She is a pseudo-intellectual noodle who will trade her birthright for a brief moment of cerebral glory.

A variation of this approach is frequently used on actresses, dancers, singers, painters, writers, and musicians —any girl who has dedicated herself to one of the Muses. After expressing profound respect for her talents, a man will declare that in order to fulfil herself as an artist it is essential that she understand LIFE. To understand LIFE she

 Girls! Girls! That scrap of paper is all the security you have in the world!

must live deeply and fully. And this, of course, can mean only one thing—without which, she is told, her work will be uninspired and meaningless. She will not be a *real artist*.

The sensitive soul cannot stand up against such intellectualizing, and rare is the creative female who is not willing to make the supreme sacrifice for Art.

LINE NUMBER TWELVE

## *The Spiritual Approach*

This is a reverse logic, far-fetched, unorthodox kind of Line, and it seems incredible anyone would attempt to use it. Yet the man who uses it does so with great success on girls who are indifferent to the various conventional approaches of his friends.

Acknowledging the presence of an overwhelming attraction between him and the girl, this man permits the subject of marriage to be broached. He refuses, however to commit himself, on the following grounds:

Being of an intensely spiritual nature, he is determined that his marriage shall be based on a tender feeling rooted in the compatibility of two souls. And since his physical reaction to her is of a particularly ardent sort, he is apprehensive. He fears his love may be nothing more than a screen for the vile passion of desire, and to marry for such a reason is most repugnant to him. Only by satisfying his desire and, so to speak, getting it out of the way, can he see what is left, and judge whether their union can exist on a sufficiently lofty plain.

What folly to listen to such reasoning! Even if he were sincere, it might be a matter of ten years before he had cooled enough to make an accurate appraisal of his love.

Number Twelve is off the beaten track, a Line you are not likely to meet. Not often do men achieve their low purpose by using such high-minded arguments. I submit it here merely as an oddity, a curiously interesting example of an original—a veritable *coup de sexe*.

## LINE NUMBER THIRTEEN

### *Like a Father to You*

The protagonist here is usually old enough to be your father, and sometimes old enough to be your father's father. Elderliness in itself is not a vice, but when it misuses its prerogatives to trap trusting young girls, one cannot help but feel indignant. Somehow, the pursuit of the petticoat is more becoming to youth.

The nice bald or whitehaired gentleman who is "enchanted by your sweet manners"—who has "a daughter your age," and who likes "to be with young people" is just as dangerous as a boy of eighteen. It is his custom to throw you off guard with a kind, fatherly manner. When he puts his elderly arm around your shoulders, you suppose he is merely leaning on you for support. You are sure you must be imagining it when the pressure of his embrace increases. You ask yourself, "How can he mean anything? He'd be shocked to know such an idea entered my mind."

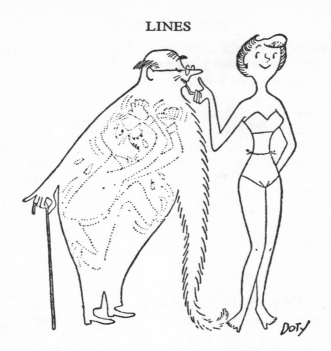

So you smile in a fond, daughterly way, and he responds with a squeeze, or even oops!—a pinch. Again the wicked thought comes to you. "Maybe—? No, no—he's only being jolly."

Then he kisses you with paternal tenderness, and you dare not pull away, for fear of offending the nice old man. If you do not object to the first kiss, how can you stop him at the second or third or fourth, even though their flavour is gradually changing? By the time his intentions become unmistakable, you have given in to so many hugs, squeezes, pats, pecks and kisses, that it is difficult to go back and put your relationship on an innocent basis.

Can you tell him it's all a mistake. Can you say you thought he was being fatherly, and wound his poor old heart? After all, at his age he must be harmless—you hope. He only wants to play at being young again. And if you are at all sentimental, you will find it most difficult to extricate yourself from his embraces. This he is counting

71

THE UNFAIR SEX

on and he will make every effort to push his advantage all the way. For he is not playing at all. He *means* it.

It is amusing to note that, invariably, when you resist this man, he becomes indignant. He pretends to believe you were leading him on. Do not let this confuse you. Be strong. Be ruthless. Have no respect for his years.

It is best, of course, to stop him before he gets started. Often you can recognize his number by the trend of his conversation. He is prone to criticize young men—they are unmannerly, uncouth, they don't understand women, and where is one worthy of such a darling as you? He extolls the virtues of maturity—the stability, wealth, and prestige which come only with the accumulation of years.

Do not eliminate anyone as being too fine to use this Line. Neither a man's dignity nor his position places him beyond suspicion. He may be your father's friend, your mother's cousin, your boy-friend's uncle, your teacher, your preacher, your boss, your doctor, your dentist, or your member of parliament—if he claims he feels like a father to you, and behaves much more affectionately than most fathers do—beware! There are young ideas whirling around in that old grey head.

In the same age-group, there is another kind of man. This one does not pretend to feel the least bit paternal. He gives and asks no quarter. He is as vigorous and lusty as a man in his forties, and as free in his choice of a Line. His chances for success are great, since he has the advantage of long years of experience, and he has acquired a knack of doing things the easy way. Such a man is often quite attractive, possessing the charm of a fine antique, plus a kind of eternal virility.

For them I have a certain reluctant admiration—they at least are no less honest and above-board than other men. It is the pseudo papas and the foxy grandpas who should be put out of business.

# LINES

## LINE NUMBER FOURTEEN

### *Mother Me*

This Line is used by young men on women who **are** older than they are, and by elderly boys, i.e., men **who** have a boyish quality.

They seldom try for a very young girl, depending as **they** do on the strong maternal instinct of Woman. Nor **will** they waste time on an inexperienced one, since they **also** rely on a generous disposition, and a generous woman **is** rarely inexperienced.

The man who uses Number Fourteen knows to **what** extent a woman's maternal emotions are stirred when she looks into his big blue brown green or grey eyes. He knows how dear he looks when his pretty curly or straight hair **is** tousled. He knows how winsome his smile is, how **boyish** his frown. He is just a great big child. And the bigger **and** brawnier, the more appealing he is in this role.

He will make sure to know less than you do about **a** great many matters. He will seek your advice, **your** approval, your praise. His caresses will be a little bit **shy,** his advances respectful and tentative. He is a child lost in **a** man's world. Dear boy, you think, he doesn't dare. **It** isn't fair. You remember the others, bold and demanding, who got what they wanted. This one is only waiting to be loved. Ah, the darling!

The mother in you cries out, "Give this innocent what he needs and longs for." Like a beneficent goddess you open your arms and fold him to your bosom. Presto! How quickly, how suddenly the little boy becomes a full-grown man.

Tsk!

## LINE NUMBER FIFTEEN

### *For Medicinal Purposes Only*

An overt threat to sever relations and a covert appeal for compassion are combined in F.M.P.O. The balance is so delicate that it would be rather difficult to describe the manoeuvre in theory. I therefore give you the following as a practical demonstration of how it is done:

SCENE: Your living room.
TIME: Any

You: What's the matter?

He: (moodily) Nothing.

You: You seem so depressed lately.

He: No—it's nothing—I'm just tired.

You: Maybe you're not getting enough sleep.

He: (with a rueful little laugh) I wouldn't be surprised. I haven't been able to sleep for weeks.

You: But that's terrible! Maybe it's your stomach.

He: It can't be. I hardly eat anything.

You: (hesitantly) Now don't get angry, but—don't you think maybe you've been drinking too much?

He: Much too much. But that's not the cause—it's the effect.

You: You really ought to see a doctor.

He: Oh, I've seen one.

You: What did he say? (He shrugs his shoulders.) Well, what?

He: Nothing—nothing. What's the use? A doctor can't help me.

You: But what—? (Wearily he draws you to him and kisses you. Then fiercely he holds you away from him, making deep finger marks on your arms.)

He: I'm going home. (He releases you abruptly.)

You: So early?

He: You'll have to excuse me. I—

You: (sympathetically) Of course. I understand.

He: (with a rueful little laugh) Do you? I wonder. (You look puzzled.) Look—maybe we'd better not see each other any more. You're a sweet girl, and I'm crazy about you. Only—

You: Only what?

He: (looking at you, broodingly) Only—you don't know what you're doing to me. (He makes more deep finger-marks on your arms. Then abruptly he pushes you away.)

You: What? What is it?

He: (He shakes his head and looks deep into your eyes.) I can't go on like this. I won't be good for anything. I've got to think of my health—my mental and physical health.

You: Why don't you see a different doc—

He: (interrupting you) I don't need a doctor. (He looks deep into your eyes. He makes finger-marks. Then abruptly he pushes you away. This time he starts for the door, and you go after him impulsively.)

You: (You are gripped by a horrible feeling of guilt. What have you done to him! Have you a right to think only of yourself, you wonder? No, no. This boy needs you. He really, honestly *needs* you.) WAIT! Come back! (He comes back—not for selfish or flighty reasons—but For Medicinal Purposes Only.)

Dear Girl, your best bet is to shake him—but well.

# THE UNFAIR SEX

## *Confidence Game*

*"Beware lest you lose the substance by grasping at the shadow."*
—AESOP

There are some men who know that they have little to offer a woman. They are too old or too unattractive or too nondescript—or married. Justifiably or not, they feel there is no chance of success if they rely on their personal appeal, and they therefore use promises of money, gifts, or opportunities, as a decoy to win over innocent girls.

No man who is small enough to employ these methods is big enough to fulfil his promises. What he does is to dwell at such length on the things he will buy for you and do for you, that you come to feel as if the good deeds were already done.

And so you are liberal with your favours. For how can one refuse anything to so kind a benefactor? Would it not seem crude to "hold out" until you have received some tangible evidence of his generosity? The black-hearted knave who uses this Line hopes you will reason thus. Putting up no collateral, he goes deep into your debt, safe in the knowledge that you cannot force payment. And the ambitious girl allows herself to be trapped by these tactics again and again.

This strategy is particularly efficacious—and therefore widely used—in connection with career girls in the theatre, the arts, the professions, and even in business—any place where contacts and influence are of prime importance in attaining success. But rarely is it employed by the man who is in a position to help you, for his kind is very busy—warding off the hundreds of girls who, like you, seek to use him. As a matter of pride, the important man wants to win you on his own merits. Full of the neuroses that accompany success, he has to be convinced you want him for himself, and not for your personal advancement.

Generally it is some underling with no real power who promises to "get" you something. Actually, all he intends to "get" is you. The introduction to a top man somehow never comes off. The opportunity to help you somehow never arrives. You find out—too late, of course—that he cannot or will not do anything for you.

Learn to recognize the empty ring to the Confidence Man's promises—the vagueness and improbability of his plans for you. The man who wants to, and expects to, and is able to make life easier for you will not find it necessary to tell you all about it in advance, like someone holding out to a child the promise of rewards for good behaviour. The truly generous man will give first—freely and graciously—in the hope of receiving in turn the harvest of your honest gratitude.

## LINE NUMBER SEVENTEEN

### *Eat, Drink, and Be Merry*

Number Seventeen has a certain unpretentious charm. The wretch who uses it does not expend a great deal of energy wearing you down with statistics and arguments. His manner is light, debonair, sophisticated, and he pretends that the realm of the physical has no importance. It is a bubble, a bauble, a bonbon, a delicious, delectable delight.

In the face of his winning insouciance, you would feel like an insufferable stick-in-the-mud if you dissented. To speak such words as "Propriety," "Decency," "Morality," would seem almost vulgar. Besides, his is a charming philosophy and you are rather taken in with it.

He warms to the receptive glow in your eye. He hails you as a fellow-traveller who rises above the tears and

turmoil of living to gather the sweet tender rosebuds.*
Here are two adult people with the right attitude towards
life. Well met! With disarming nonchalance he puts his
head on your lap, and sighing an abandoned sigh, mur-
murs something about the absurdity of taking oneself
seriously . . . and how insignificant we are in the im-
mensity of the universe. Kissing you casually, he asks,
"What difference will anything make a thousand years
from now? Why deny yourself life's little pleasures?"

Why, indeed? How worldy it all seems. How you yearn
to be merry and prove yourself the perfect companion-
piece to this golden boy. With your mind adjusted to the
perspective of a thousand years, you completely lose sight
of tomorrow's tears.

LINE NUMBER EIGHTEEN

## The Expert

This is a tantalizing Line, and one that depends for its
success on the natural curiosity of Woman. The man who
uses it declares that sex is the most wonderful, most
exciting expression of life, and that the practice of it is a
divine art. However (he tells you), most men are not
equipped for the correct practice of this art—their education is sketchy, their skill woefully inadequate. But you are
fortunate. Here is a man who has made a profound study
of the subject, one who has a natural talent and has
developed it to the highest degree of proficiency. He
possesses voluptuous secrets, he can introduce you to
exquisite pleasures, he has the key that opens mystic doors
to undreamed-of wonders. He is willing, nay, eager to
teach you all he knows.

"Gather ye rosebuds while ye may" is a scandalous bit
of advice which Robert Herrick addressed "To the virgins
to make much of time" in the seventeenth century. Obviously
he spoke to advance the interests of his own sex. Furthermore his
advice is impracticable—for how many rosebuds can a virgin gather?
One rosebud and you're out.

# LINES

Tutored in ancient lore by a Javanese temple-girl, initiated into the Seven Great Mysteries by an Andalusian princess, owner of the rare third volume of the Chinese Bibliotheque Erotica, veteran of two years in an Arabian harem and three months in Hollywood—this is a man such as you will surely never meet again.

You are intrigued, fascinated, stimulated, and devoured by a desire for knowledge. You beg him to lift just a tiny corner of the veil. But not one peek will he give away. These lessons are not taught by word of mouth.

You are goaded by curiosity. You conjecture. You speculate. You cannot conceive of anything so marvellous as the treasure he is offering. You send your mind off in a hundred directions and it comes back empty-handed. You cannot bear the suspense, the not knowing. You tell yourself that if you let this opportunity slip by, you will worry all your life about what you have missed.

Bewitched, captivated, and entranced, you surrender to the mystery and the dazzle of his abracadabra.

Ho hum.

\*     \*     \*

Learn the Lines as if they were popular tunes, which in a manner of speaking they are. Become so familiar with each one that you can easily recognize the melody in the dark. It is a great comfort to be able to label a man as number so-and-so or such-and-such. It reduces him to a known quantity and removes the glamour and the mystery which make him so hard to resist.

Let him sing. It would be rude to stop him or say you have heard that one before. Hum along with him if you like. But—do not let yourself be carried away. Keep busy with destructive thoughts. Ask yourself: How often has he used this line? How many times has it been successful? Does he think I'm falling for it? Am I? Will I be sorry tomorrow? Is it worth it? In this way you may counteract the effectiveness of his siren song and resist the temptation to give yourself.

## CHAPTER SIX

# Devices

SOMETIMES a man does not rely on words alone to win his point. Instead he utilizes some extraneous device, such as costume, music, props, or contrived situation. Quite often he does no more than expose the female to the Device, and she—like the romantic nightingale who impaled itself on the thorns of a rose—embraces the very means of her destruction.

Here again, space permits me to give only a few examples:

### The Uniform

This device is used every day by the men in our Army, Navy and Air Force. It is common knowledge among fighting men that the trim fit of military apparel has the same effect on a woman as a well-made love-potion—that there is a strong female affinity for the neat, the meticulous, the braid and the brass. Moreover, the man in uniform has something more than a pretty suit of clothes. He has an aura, a strong male-ish flavour which comes of being segregated in an excessively masculine atmosphere for long periods of time. This emanation draws women as honey draws bears. Add it to the glamorous halo of travel, danger, and officers' clubs, and it is easy to understand why these men are practically irresistible.

There is a strong pull on feminine curiosity here, too. You cannot help but wonder and wonder and wonder how he looks out of uniform, for otherwise how can you tell whether it is the man or the outward trappings that makes your heart go pitapat? It is a lost cause when a girl longs to see a man in his underwear.

It is not necessary for him to do more than hint at his longing for you, mention the stern call of duty which will carry him away so soon, and imply that you could give him a beautiful memory to take with him. You are struck by the self-restraint, the sacrificial spirit of this man, whose life is dedicated to defending you and yours—and there rises in you a fervent wish to give him an hour of peace in this war-mad world. Here is the perfect excuse to give way, for the sternest conscience cannot disprove that what you want to do is actually unselfish and patriotic.

An experienced Soldier, Sailor, Airman, etc., can quickly sniff the scent of victory when he sees that exalted look of self-abnegation in your eyes. For the *coup de grace* he gives you a fragment of his uniform—his wings, his insignia—or just a button—as a farewell remembrance, and you are spurred into action. You realize with a rush that there is no time to ponder, to weigh the pros and cons, to dilly-dally. The pressure of time is upon you, and with your hero's token clutched in your hand, you hasten to add one more trinket to his collection of military souvenirs.

There are other uniforms, besides the military, designed to make a girl lose her perspective. The female is ever enchanted by the romantic figure of a mounted policeman, a drum major, a lion tamer, a fireman, or any other ordinary male encased in the splendid armour of his calling. She would do well to realize that it matters not how attractive he looks—he is still the enemy.

We must learn to appraise each man quite apart from his outer covering.

# DEVICES
## *The Portrait*

The camera and the easel are formidable weapons. When an artist asks you to pose for him, you cannot help but find it an extraordinary compliment—even if he is an amateur. In the professional atmosphere of his studio, a man acquires many privileges. Should he ask you to remove your blouse, he is within his artistic rights. And if he spends long minutes adjusting a drape around your shoulders, tugging at a strap here and tucking in a ribbon there, you can hardly complain unless his hands are cold. It is the customary procedure to study you, pose you, sketch you, tire you, and ultimately topple you from your pedestal.

Photographers, too, are always looking for new subjects, and they use exactly the same processing, with the added refinement of a darkroom. If you do go to have your picture taken—watch the man and not the birdie.

## *The Musicale*

This is a charming device in which the man works on your sensitivity to music. He sings to you in a soft and vibrant voice, while his strong fingers pluck spine-tingling sounds out of a deep-throated guitar. Or he woos you with African drums, or with a zither, or with some other effective instrument. Even a man with no musical talent whatsoever may include this routine in his repertoire—he simply uses a record player, which has the compensating virtue of being self-operating. The musical host always provides atmosphere—a moonlit beach, a drifting canoe, a campfire in the woods, or some other stock setting. If he is obliged to entertain indoors, he turns down the lights and invites you to relax on the floor amid some cushions.

Music has an unfortunate effect on a woman's emotions, and a well-programmed concert can hardly fail of its objective. *If I Loved You ... Smoke Gets In Your Eyes ... Some Enchanted Evening ... Bolero ... Moonlight Sonata ... One Night of Love ... Kiss Me Again ...* If you are at all aesthetic, you cannot but be stirred to your depths, and by the time *Ah, Sweet Mystery of Life* sneaks up on you, you are saturated with the exquisite beauty of it all. You want to laugh or cry or dance or swoon—or do something. Your hand seeks his, his lips find yours, together you soar on wings of song—Music Lovers.

### The Troo-de-Loo*

The meanest Device employed by man is the one of isolating you in a selected locale from which there is no escape. Giving no sign of his vile intentions, the man who has plotted a troo-de-loo lures you, all unsuspecting, into a fateful trap.

For example, after an innocent picnic in the country, you find yourself stranded for the night on a deserted road—in a car that will not budge. If he has no car, he contrives to lose the way on foot, blundering about until darkness overtakes you some place far from human habitation.

Or he takes you boating in a small sail or power boat— just the two of you, of course—and because of mechanical difficulties, or tides, or some such thing, you are marooned for the night in the middle of the bay or sound or lake.

If you go canoeing by moonlight, he stops off on one of those little islands that dot the waterways, and the canoe floats off, as canoes do, leaving the two of you to wait for the sunrise.

If he is too lazy to plan an excursion, he may manoeuvre you into staying past the closing hour in an office, store, school or library. There are many unrecorded cases of a building being locked for the night with some unsuspecting female caught inside with a scheming male.

All these are troo-de-loos—highly seasoned, perilous, explosive. The hazards of spending a whole night alone with a man whose intentions are amorous cannot be

 Actually *trou-de-loup* (French), *trou*: hole, *de*: of, *loup*: wolf.

exaggerated. The time passes slowly, there is little you can do to amuse yourself, and, as is well-known, the body reaches its lowest ebb of resistance in the hours before dawn.

There is, unhappily, no way of anticipating a troo-de-loo. It is absurd to refuse all invitations for driving, hiking, flying and boating, though actually that would be the only real safeguard. But there are certain precautions a girl can take. For one thing, never start out on an excursion without full cosmetic equipment. Your worry and discomfort, should you be trapped, will be eased greatly by the knowledge that you can put on fresh make-up whenever you please. There is no reason why you should not look your best at all times, and never will you have more need of artificial aids than during a night spent *al fresco*.

Another preparedness measure is to carry a pack of cards and a small torch concealed in your handbag. When you realize you are in a troo-de-loo, you can distract him and keep your own mind off other things, with a brisk game of gin rummy or poker.* The torch is a great boon, for besides throwing light on the cards, it helps counteract the romantic innuendoes of darkness.

This card and torch kit is not guaranteed to save you, but at any rate it serves as a delaying action. And it makes a girl feel that at least she tried.

A far more effective method of protection, but one which few girls make the effort to employ, is to study astronomy, geography, navigation and engines. If you know how to fix any mechanical gadget, if you can plot a course by the stars, if you have the instincts of a homing pigeon, you are the girl who can foil the man who gets you into a troo-de-loo.

 Be sure the stakes are *clearly defined*, and do not risk anything you cannot well afford to lose.

It is apparent that men may accomplish a great deal without the use of Lines. I cannot admonish you too strongly to be on the alert when the familiar words are not forthcoming. There is no way of knowing from which direction the attack will come, as a man can convert the most innocent circumstances into an instrument of seduction.

## *The Ring*

It is rather shocking, but nevertheless true, that a man will use the symbol of his good faith as a device to get the best of his promised bride. And she, mellowed and softened by the good fortune of her betrothal, is an easy target for his ignoble intentions.

For, what girl can suspect a male of treachery while his diamond sparkles on her finger? The most impertinent suggestions seem only reasonable when proposed by the darling who has publicly contracted to marry her. She loses sight of the fact that he is still a man and thinks of him only as her future husband.

Too many short-sighted maidens, mistaking the promise for the deed, have prematurely unveiled the final mystery. What a pity that anyone clever enough to lead a man within shooting distance of the altar should, at the last minute, be undone by the very token which heralded her coming triumph.

# DEVICES

The engagement ring is no substitute for the wedding ring. Until you have the certificate in hand, you are not safely home, for even the most frugal man is capable of forfeiting his deposit.

## The Twenty-four Carat Toy

Some men are endowed with natural advantages, such as imported cars or yachts or country estates or membership in exclusive clubs, or other assets less costly but equally alluring. All such attributes rank high as devices because women understandably attach much value to being seen in the right places, or enjoying the envy of other women, and on sampling luxuries they cannot afford and never expect to own.

The man who uses this device does not offer some extravagancy as a gift, or even as a loan. He simply flaunts it and inflames the female with a desire to share the use of it. If he is at all subtle, he never mentions the toll he will levy for granting her this taste of high life. He knows that the luxury-loving female who is dazzled by his twenty-four carat toy will refuse him nothing, so eager is she to be invited to come and play again.

Is it not sad to think that there are girls who are willing to pay so dearly for a pleasure which is only transient?

## CHAPTER SEVEN

# Techniques

THE technician never urges, begs, or coerces. His is a carefully thought-out campaign of action, calculated to induce you to yield without giving battle. Because nothing is done to engender opposition, you are deprived of an opportunity to defend yourself, and in fact, as a result of clever manipulation

 *You may actually find yourself in the position of aggressor.*

The most representative Techniques are The Body Technique, The Dearest-Enemies Technique, The Open-Hand, The Strong-Arm, The Liquor, The Gibraltar, and The Oblique, and this is how they operate:

## The Body Technique

Here we have a rudimentary, almost primitive example. Swift, simple, direct, it does not concern itself with the mental processes but relies on the high animal spirits of the healthy female. And as it is rather strenuous it is most popular among the very young.

The preferred setting is the beach or country, although it is often staged successfully indoors. Ostensibly begun in a spirit of fun, the Body Technique engages the immediate and innocent co-operation of any friendly girl.

If no natural opening presents itself, such as a useless article he can start a scuffle over or a lake he can duck you in, the boy leads off by demonstrating his superior strength in some way, like picking you up and carrying you, or squeezing your hand until you scream. He then invites you to squeeze his, and when you try, he is amused by your feminine lack of strength. Pretending to resent this, you prove what a great big girl you are by proceeding to hit him, scratch him, bite him, kick him, pull his hair, strangle him, grapple, wrestle and tangle with him. In return he will squeeze you, trip you, and sit on you, he will tickle you, smother you, pinch you, exhaust you, get a scissors hold on you, a toe hold, a leg hold, a head hold, and force your shoulders to the ground. And there you are.

If you would play safe, avoid wrestling and other sports which bring you into close contact with one of the opposite sex. There is no foretelling what may come of the accidental juxtaposition of two bodies.

### The Dearest-Enemies Technique

The attention of a woman can sometimes be arrested by a man who withholds all compliments and shows no interest at all. In fact, a clever man can, by looking the other way, provoke an attractive girl into throwing herself at him. This, however, is rare and presupposes a fundamental magnetism on the part of the man.

More common is the Dearest-Enemies Technique. Here

the man is not indifferent. He is actively disagreeable and sometimes insulting. This brings him sharply to your notice, and as you examine him you observe that he is polite and charming to everyone but you. You are hurt. What is there about you that should earn his dislike? You dislike him in return.

You discover he thinks you are conceited, or spoiled, or too sure of yourself, and this pleases you, for such criticisms imply a kind of admiration. How unbearable if he'd said you were silly, or boring, or bony!

It surprises you that this man so often finds it necessary to be near you, as if for the very pleasure of being sarcastic and even rude. Sometimes he is aloof. He stares at you from a distance, with a sardonic smile, as if he has some secret information about you. The antagonism between you grows so strong that your pulse quickens at the mere sight of him, and you look forward with a savage joy to exchanging verbal cruelties.

There is a time and tide in these affairs. When the friction between you reaches the point where little sparks begin to fly, he will know the moment for action has arrived. Whereupon he will seize you and kiss you angrily, fiercely. "He *loves* me!" your soul cries out in triumph.

Why, then, was he so mean? Reluctantly, the dragon confesses he was fighting the attraction you had for him. He was fighting it because—

He thought you didn't care for him, or

He thought you were like other women, and he didn't want to be hurt again, or

He was afraid he might hurt you, or

He knew you belonged to Ted, or—

Whatever the reason, he can resist you no longer!

The abrupt change of mood, the astounding revelation, the delicious flattery and excitement of it all combine to throw you off balance. All your defences fall down. You become putty in his hands. You are lost, lost, lost!

Sometimes a man does not utilize the impetuous kiss at

the peak of hostilities. Instead he suddenly stops fighting, runs his fingers through his hair, and with a haunted look, manoeuvres you into asking what is wrong. Then he reveals that "he can't go on like this"—"he's mad for you"—"he's been fighting the attraction because"— etcetera, etcetera as listed above, with similar results, i.e., putty.

This Technique is so common that it is frequently used as the basic plot of magazine stories, plays, and movies. One cannot be too sure whether this is an instance of art imitating life or life imitating art. At any rate, do not be misled by the fact that in these fictional stories the couple invariably gets married. Real life is not as strictly censored as our entertainment.

## The Open-Hand Technique

The Open-Hand is the least reprehensible of all Techniques. He who is willing to spend his time and money freely in order to win a girl is the most lovable kind of male. It is not surprising that he is also the most admired by women, despite the fact that he is seldom young or attractive.

The Open-Handed man does not make a lot of empty promises. Nor does he ask you what you would like, so that in stating your desires you feel as if you have made a request. Instead, he gives you little things, like flowers or chocolates or perfume or some trinket or trifle he knows you want.

If he is very wealthy he may buy you a house or some diamonds or fine furs. Most customarily given is the Mink Coat which has come to symbolize this kind of man in the minds of most girls.*

The givers of these more valuable gifts and attentions are remarkably scarce. Where they do crop up, they are usually the victims of extreme, personalized desire, or unreasoning love. However, few girls have the wherewithal to command such tribute, and even those who have, seldom are lucky enough to get it.

And if he is influential, he pulls strings for you and cuts corners to help you prosper in your social or business career.

It is very easy to become accustomed to good things, and in no time at all, you find yourself completely dependent on this man's kindness. Moreover, it is impossible not to develop a deep affection for one who is so generous. Under these conditions, it would seem ungrateful, insensitive, even unreasonable to withhold what he so palpably has earned. Every woman past the age of sixteen knows what is expected of her under these conditions, and it is extremely unethical to take unless you intend to give. After all, *noblesse oblige!*

If ever you are fortunate enough to meet and attract this kind of man, your only defence will be to refuse all his gifts and favours. Unless you do so you will have no justification for refusing yours to him.

## *The Strong-Arm Technique*

With a minimum of flattery and no tricks at all, the Strong-Arm man makes a direct lunge the first or second time he dates you.

Usually he is attractive, and, operating on the assumption that he is irresistible, he disdains any pretence at courtship. Quite often he is merely a crude, direct person with neither the inclination nor the ability to woo a woman properly.

In either case, his motto is, "You can't get killed for trying." And he quite sensibly estimates that the law of averages will take care of him, for if only fifty per cent of his attempts are successful, he is still way ahead of the game. Often he makes the attempt not because he really wants you, or thinks he will succeed, but because it is an amusing and inexpensive way to pass the time, and a matter of principle with him to try on every occasion.

It is his habit to depend entirely on physical action and reaction. He proceeds briskly, as if he takes it for granted that you will acquiesce. The effect this has on a girl is devastating. Somehow there is no room for hesitation. She is not faced with the necessity of making a decision, or embarrassed by timid advances that call for protest. All responsibility is taken away from her, and this puts her conscience quietly to rest. She need do nothing more than let go and float with the tide. Ah well! Human beings are ever prone to surrender to a force which is stronger than they are and knows where it is going.

Nine times out of ten, you will not hear from this type again *regardless whether you accept or reject him*. If he is rejected, he thinks of all the girls who have been willing in the past and will be willing in the future, and he blithely decides not to waste any time on you. If he is accepted, he is pleased with himself, but feels no particular warmth for you in the afterglow. In short order, he will forget you, your name, and your generosity. It is, of course, possible that he will date you again, once or twice, depending on how many new girls he meets, and his percentage of successes. But this is meagre return for what you have given, and the aftermath is invariably bitter or, at the very least, disappointing.

It would seem that any female, no matter how inexperienced or how eager, would have better sense than to succumb to this Strong-Arm method. It is damaging to her in particular, and to the female sex in general. Yet men say they are continually surprised by the frequency with which the Technique works. Apparently there are far too many foolish girls who give in without ado. And the saddest aspect of the whole business is that the same girls fall for it over and over again, telling themselves each time, "This will be different."

There is always *some* consolation to be found *somewhere* for a girl who falls for any other method of intrigue, but I have not one word of cheer to offer a girl who takes the insult direct lying down.

# TECHNIQUES

## *The Liquor Technique*

Why does a man coax you to have another and another and still another drink, when obviously you can hold no more? Because he needs a drinking partner? Ridiculous. In that case he would seek a male companion who could pay his own way. No—when a man badgers you into drinking too much, it is for the purpose of rendering you witless and feckless. He knows that alcohol slows down your reactions and destroys your inhibitions, and that if he can induce you to drink enough you will be easy prey for any mischief he has in mind.

Some men use liquor only as a crutch, depending on it to aid them in conjunction with some other Method of

Intrigue. This is the Quasi-Liquor Stratagem under which a man urges you to drink only enough to make you feel a bit light-headed and open-handed. In this state your perspective is distorted, boundaries and limitations recede in a haze of careless good humour, and you are in no mood for argument. You give in happily on every point, and end up by allowing him to win you over with comparative ease. This method is almost as underhanded as its big brother, the Liquor Technique.*

For the kind of man who plies you with drink and throws you for a loss when you are quite senseless, I have not one kind word. His is the way of a lazy man and a coward, a villain and a pickpocket. Shun him, for he has no honour and no shame.

## *The Gibraltar Technique*

It is the man of leisurely nature, patient and stubborn, who will go to the trouble of using this tedious system. He is the sort who will not settle for second or third best, but prefers to hang on to his original choice despite rebuffs and discouragements. I have known cases where men actually persevered for three or four years!

This hardy fellow hovers in the background while you move from one infatuation to another. He stands, always ready, hopeful of catching you on the rebound. He will nurse you through a broken heart, and help you with your income-tax, and fill in when you have no date, and massage your feet when they are tired after dancing with someone else. He is always there when you need him, this sturdy rock.

In his spare time he may well be amusing himself with other girls, less difficult to please. But he never permits these side-issues to interfere with his main project. He is gambling that one day you will be so fatigued, or so disillusioned, or so weakened by the vicissitudes of life that

Neither should be confused, however, with the perfectly permissible gesture of offering one or two genteel drinks to a young lady in order to "break the ice," as the saying goes.

you will suddenly look at him, realize how comfortable he is, and fall gratefully into his arms.

Or it may be his hope that the biological moment will arrive when you needs must belong to someone, and nobody else being immediately available, you will settle for Old Faithful.

Or, who knows? the time may come when you feel you must reward him for his loyalty and dependability—as one might throw a dog a bone.

In any event, he cares not what the reason, so long as he gains that upon which he has trained his sights.

Do not feel too smug about this dear old friend. Do not scoff at the idea that some day he may get you. He has every chance of succeeding. For he is usually an inferior quality second-grade male, the kind no woman fears or wants, and with him you are relaxed—confident you will not do anything silly.

This is a fatal state of mind. Inevitably the moment must come when your attention will wander. There will be a new moon, or an old, familiar tune, and before you can catch yourself, he will have gathered you up and slipped you over the brink.

### The Oblique Technique

The man who uses this one is either attractive or charming or both. He possesses patience and perfect self-control. *And* he understands women. A female who is at all susceptible to masculine wiles does not stand a chance against him.

This man will make himself most agreeable in every way. He never fails to phone when you expect him to, or even when you do not expect him to. He dates you with pleasing regularity. Without giving you a "rush" he manages to make you feel flattered and courted. *But*—he does not kiss you.

It is most upsetting when a man does not behave according to form. What is a girl to think if she is with a man who likes her, and they arrive at the moment that calls for a kiss, their first kiss—what is she to think in this familiar situation if he acts in an unfamiliar way? There you are, with your refusal or acceptance at the tip of your pretty pink tongue, and no attempt is made. The first time this happens, you are mildly surprised, but as other such moments come and go and come and go, a cloud of bewilderment settles over you.

Bewilderment breeds anxiety, anxiety breeds loss of self-confidence, and this in turn causes a general inability to think clearly, So, by doing nothing, the man reduces you to a shaky and vulnerable state.

Not content with these results, he works concurrently on another angle. By careful contrivance, the circumstances surrounding your dates are always such as to turn your thoughts to love and kisses. This unprincipled male will drive you out to the country to watch a sunset—and he will *watch the sunset*, oblivious of the happy couples in other parked cars. There will be long, long hours of sitting in a hammock on a dark porch, or lying silent on a beach or on a hill or in front of an open fire—and he will come so close that you are *almost* touching, and yet he will be careful not to touch so much as your little finger.

This man is like a gardener, watching a fruit as it hangs on the tree. Day after day he nurtures it and admires it, but, exercising tremendous self-discipline, he neither feels it, nor pinches it, nor tests it to see if it is ready. And then, one day, he holds out his hand and the fruit simply drops into it, ripe and warm and eager to be eaten.

Just so, by the time you have had your fourth, sixth, or eighth date with a man who makes the oblique attack, you will have reached the boiling point, and he will know it. The dénouement is sweet and inevitable. He need but look tenderly into your eyes, press your shoulders gently toward him, and—pfff!

There is No Defence. The only way of escape is FULL RETREAT the instant you recognize the earmarks of his deadly technique.

A word of advice to those stubborn maidens who will insist on engaging in a finish fight with such an adversary despite all that I have here set forth:

Do not ask him, "Why haven't you kissed me?" or "Exactly how do you feel about me?" Even if you word these questions cleverly, he will know what you are getting at, and you will be put in the embarrassing position of having openly provoked him to kiss you (or what is commonly known as "asking for it").

And do not, *please do not attack him.* You have got to outwait him. Be patient. Force yourself. He knows the struggle you are having and is doing everything he can to make it harder for you. Unfortunately, not every girl has the stamina to hold out. Each year more and more of you fail in this respect. It is my hope that we can reverse the trend, and with that goal in mind, I give you this talisman:

     *If you wait, he will try.*

If you must go down in defeat, let it be with a minimum of dishonour.

## CHAPTER EIGHT

# International Relations

*"Love your neighbour, but don't take down your fence."*
—SANDBURG

THE same Lines, Devices, and Techniques are used by civilized men all over the world. Our girls do not seem to realize this fact. Hundreds succumb every year to such superficial accoutrements as a cute accent, a quaint name, or a fur-lined overcoat. *Mademoiselle* or *Senorita* or *Fräulein* sounds so much more respectful than Toots or Babe, that the man who uses the foreign form of salutation seems incapable of low motives.

When a man named Jacques, for instance, listens to you with bewildered concentration, then says in his best Boyer accents, "Mademoiselle, you weel come 'ome with me, non? There eet ees quiet—also I have 'ome the Anglo-French deectionaire—and we can talk, non?"—you are likely to say oui oui if you know any French at all. Surely things are different in his country, you think. There, a nice girl may go to a man's apartment without inviting trouble. One sees it in their films all the time. When a woman of the world enters, she simply lets her coat drop to the floor,

100

and he *knows*. But if it is a nice girl she keeps her coat on until he takes it from her and hangs it tenderly on a hook. Then they speak in low caressing tones, they drink wine, he kisses her hand a few times, and after a while he takes her home on his bicycle. Ah, how lovely to be such a girl and get your hand kissed in this adorable man's apartment.

Actually, his aims, attitude, and motivations are identical with those of the guy named Jack who squeezes your knees under the table and says, "What do you say, honey —let's get away from this racket and go up to my place, where we can talk!" But an odd accent and new inflection have a way of imbuing the most worn-out words with a kind of freshness.

The plea that sex is beautiful, when voiced by a platinum-blond Scandinavian with noble blue eyes and the body of a Viking, or by a rugged, wholesome-looking Dutchman, takes on an authenticity which makes it difficult to scoff.

The woman who is given a rush by a debonair Neapolitan or a fiery South American can hardly fail to be carried away by his enthusiasm.

If your host is a dashing Magyar, it is impossible to refuse an invitation to eat goulash, drink Tokay, and make merry according to the custom of his country.

Of course, any Line or Technique that appeals to a woman's sympathy and maternal instinct has triple appeal when offered by a boyish tenor from Ireland. And the quiet lad from Prague—so gentle, so far away from home— barely able to pronounce even your name—how can he be harbouring all sorts of schemes and wicked thoughts? Do Not Be Fooled! He is *thinking* in his *own* language.

Another advantage enjoyed by a foreigner is that it is difficult for you to understand him. By listening intently, you catch a few syllables or words such as ". . . blg . . . sridgh . . . thlznh . . . is good . . . amphgr . . . you like?"

101

All this is said with a look of bright expectancy. What is he talking about? you wonder. A book? Food? Travel? You cannot keep saying "What?" To hold up your side of the conversation, you smile understandingly and say, "Oh, yes."

*Never say Yes* unless you know exactly what the question is.

Even girls who speak several languages fluently are susceptible and easily won by men of other lands. Perhaps these linguistic young ladies *think* differently, when they converse in an alien tongue.

This is doubly true if the strangers are titled, and should

the foreigner be wearing a uniform or costume of some sort, there is practically no chance that he will be turned away. Anybody with a turban wound around his head evokes dreams of fabulous Arabian Nights. And the mere sight of a brawny Highlander in his cute little kilt is enough to cause an impressionable lass to fling herself into his arms.

What causes this? Is it a secret desire for something unknown—something mysterious? Or is it the anonymity that a girl enjoys in dallying with someone outside her own sphere?

Whatever it is, be aware that this insidious attraction exists. And remind yourself that however different his apparel, however delightful his bad English, and however lonely and lost he may seem, if he is a M-A-N he is out of the same mould as the domestic variety and is not to be trusted.

CHAPTER NINE

# How To Invite Aggression

*"Be warm, but pure; be amorous, but chaste."*—BYRON

IT is apparent that women need a well-formulated plan of defence. The theory that "a strong offence is the best defence" does not hold true in this kind of a war. Here the perfect victory* is won by inviting aggression and countering with passive resistance.

What are the qualities in a woman that attract the aggressive attentions of men? Modesty, Goodness, Tenderness, Charm, Generosity, Brightness, Mystery, Delicacy and Kindness. Let us examine these one by one.

## Modesty

Be modest about your Accomplishments. Since a reasonable amour of cleverness is necessary in attracting a man, it is a ticklish matter to maintain a proper balance in this department. Be at all times less intellectual, less

 Marriage.

witty, less successful, less proficient at games than any man you want to impress.

Be modest in your Behaviour. Try not to out-talk, out-eat, out-dress, or out-last him.

Be modest in your Apparel. You can accomplish far more by implication than by exposure. A valuable lesson can be learned from the strip-tease artist. It is not how much you show but how you show it. Do not wear short skirts unless you have good legs. Avoid low necklines unless you have a lovely bosom. Never wear short sleeves if your elbows are not pretty. In a word, conceal all defects and reveal only that which is flawless. This is true feminine modesty.

### *Goodness*

A provocative female always Smells Good and Is Good. There are two smells men love—the smell of food, and the smell of perfume. It would be absurd to suggest that you go about smelling of the kitchen, but there is no reason why you should not make full use of the sweet-smelling oils, ointments, powders, sachets, colognes and perfumes everywhere on your person.\* Do not ever leave your house, even to go to the grocery store, without putting perfume behind your knees. You never know whom you might bump into.

Be Good at whatever you do (but not too good). Do not attempt anything at which you are inefficient. Do not swim if it makes you huff and puff. Do not play tennis unless you can prance about daintily on the court. Do not dance, eat, cook, or make love, unless you can do so with agility, grace, and enthusiasm.

 "Smells are surer than sounds or sights to make your heartstrings crack."—R. KIPLING.

# HOW TO INVITE AGGRESSION
## *Tenderness*

There is something about the tenderness of a woman that goes to man's heart and exercises a never-failing lure. It brings out all the male in a male. He wants to pat, hold, kiss, touch, pinch, bite, and otherwise abuse anything that is smooth and soft.

Avoid the muscle and the stubble. Keep yourself tender!


## *Generosity*

Be gracious in bestowing small favours. You cannot continue to provoke man's interest if he has had no sample, no inkling of how sweet you are to kiss and to hold in his arms. Can he imagine how much he is missing, if he has never had the smallest taste of you?


## *Brightness*

Sequins, stardust, feathers and bows, clouds of tulle, ruffles of lace, jewels, and paint, and flowers in your hair—these fripperies may seem like an expense and a nuisance to you, but they are dear to the masculine heart. It is only among humans that the male is not privileged to be brighter than the female. And since convention forbids him to adorn himself, he can satisfy his longing for pretty things only by the vicarious joy of looking upon a decorated female.

Use all the artifices you are clever enough to manage. Men pretend they like women who look natural. Actually it is only their wives they want to see unadorned—in the hope that such protective non-colouration will discourage the attentions of other men. The girl all men turn to look at longingly is the one with the platinum hair and a smoothly applied complexion base.

# THE UNFAIR SEX

It is easy to catch a man's eye with bright and shiny objects. Like a small boy dazzled by a Christmas tree, he is impelled to come close, to examine, and to touch. So fascinated is he by the glittering ornaments, he often thinks he is in love with the tree.

## Charm

Suit your personality to the man, the occasion, the circumstances. Cultivate all sorts of synthetic traits. Be whimsical, vibrant, sophisticated, elegant, naïve, abandoned, straightforward—anything but yourself. For unless you are an unusual person, your natural, unretouched personality is likely to be as colourless as your natural unretouched complexion.

Experiment! Do not be afraid. Dare to be the woman you would like the world to think you are.

## Mystery

Never let a man know too much about you. He will like your hair less if he knows it is dyed and appreciate your smile more if he does not know your teeth are capped. Keep your age, your weight, your shoe-size, and your family squabbles to yourself. Intrigue him. Mystify him. Leave something to his imagination. Do not let him suspect that you ever have such prosaic troubles as upset stomach, running nose, or heartburn.

Nor should you let him know exactly how you feel about him. Or give out information on your past, no matter how dull it may be. Let him discover for himself just how chaste, stubborn, or naughty you are.

## Delicacy

In certain circles it is considered "modern" to enter into a physical relationship with a healthy feeling of

108

camaraderie, and to approach sex as a wholesome normal function. What could be more vulgar?

Far from being modern, this concept is older than antiquity. The Neanderthal man did not approach his female counterpart with involved schemes for overcoming her shyness. Their lovemaking was as natural and un-complicated as that of two birds, which is to say it lacked all the refinements, embellishments, and delights which civilized man has evolved over the centuries.

The mere mention of the word "wholesome" in con-nection with sex discloses a deplorable ignorance of the intricacies, the half-tones, the grace notes, the fragile mysteries and artifices which are so essential.

And to pretend that men and women are alike—what sophism is this! Do we not all know that deeply ingrained in the fundamental nature of Man is the need to conquer, to overcome—just as it is in the nature of Woman to wish to submit and be conquered? In love as in art, it is contrast and conflict that make for excitement. Be skittish, coquet-tish, reluctant, hesitant and demure—be all the things a man is not. In this Difference lies the crux of your appeal.

As to treating sex as a normal function—do not permit yourself even to think of it that way. The most exquisite nuances of romance are the flowers of inhibition, frustra-tion, guilt feelings, and forbidden dreams. The idea of putting a clear, scientific light on sex has the same aesthetic value as illuminating a moonlit lake with neon signs.

Hold on to your veils. The hidden, the forbidden, exert a terrific pull on the male.

### Kindness

The ego of a man is a wondrous tender thing. Do not bruise it. Treat it with kind and gentle understanding. Nourish it with sweet words of flattery and little marks of adoration. And if a man possess not one feature or accomplishment on which you can offer praise, invent some virtue and attribute it to him. He will not deny ownership.

More potent than compliments is an attitude of admiration. The prime function of a woman's eyes is to convey to some man her appreciation of his superior mind, body, possessions and talents.

\*　　\*

The qualities discussed in this chapter are important ones. There are others, too, more specialized, on which a woman may capitalize—as, for example, Beauty, Wealth, or Good Connections. But before deciding to develop all the traits which will make men want you, be sure that you know how to cope with popularity, for in its wake come not only blessings but also certain difficulties. Unhappily, the ability to inspire men with the desire to possess you does not carry with it the skill necessary to deflect that desire and use it to your own advantage. The most

coveted fortress is continually under attack, and must inevitably fall most often to the marauders. It is, after all, unwise to draw more fire than you can safely withstand.

Therefore each of you must determine individually how you can best utilize your assets to invite a comfortable amount of aggression—and having invited it, how you can most graciously resist it.

## CHAPTER TEN

# How To Resist a Man

*"All impediments in fancy's course are motives of more fancy."*
—SHAKESPEARE

ONLY one woman in a thousand is fortunate enough to be bothered by an excessive number of men who want to make love to her. The nine hundred and ninety-nine others, though receiving *fewer* offers, are always faced with *some* offers—and no matter how few, the discriminating girl will always come across at least one she wants to reject. Heaven forbid that you ever reach the point of no rejection.

When Man can achieve without marriage that which should be granted him only in the nuptial chamber, Woman loses her strongest weapon for forcing him into wedlock. Hold up your end! Do not be the weak link in the chain!

If you have not the vision to sacrifice selfish pleasures for the good of all womankind, you can surely find some personal reason for resisting. I recommend that you always have a good reason for resisting a man. There is no strength in an action taken "just because." It lacks conviction.

There are reasons enough to chose from:

1. You want to avoid the pangs and pains of giving.
2. The man does not appeal to you.
3. You actually cannot stand him.
4. He is married.
5. You have made up your mind to limit yourself to a certain number of men each year, and this one exceeds the quota.
6. You are in love with someone else.
7. You do not want him to have the satisfaction of chalking you up as another conquest.
8. You hope to impress him with your chastity, and thus win him for a husband. (This does not always follow. Although some men look for chastity in a wife, a frightening number marry girls who have proved themselves.)

### Practical Suggestions for Resisting

CHOICE OF LOCALE

The most important element in Resisting is Location. There are some places where it is extremely difficult for a man to make love—and other places where it is extremely difficult for him not to. Keep away from the latter whenever possible, and you will eliminate the more complicated problems which must inevitably follow.

For instance, if you are resisting, it is foolish to take your date swimming in the moonlight. He cannot swim the whole night long, and since there is little else a man can do for amusement on a dark, deserted beach, he will have no choice but to make love to you.

Avoid lonely beaches, vestibules, and country roads, sunlight, starlight, twilight, midnight, deserted classrooms, park benches, parked cars, dark hallways, hay rides and sleigh rides.

It often happens you cannot keep away from a danger

spot. The average office, for example, is a veritable hotbed. If you work in one, there is not much you can do to protect yourself. However, you can avoid working late or alone with a co-worker or executive.*

Whatever your general locale, exercise extreme caution in selecting your specific location in that locale. An apparently harmless piece of furniture can be a trap. If you sit on a hard bench, for instance, you are bound to fidget and squirm. This creates a perfect opening for your vis-à-vis to offer his lap, and if you refuse his invitation, you seem spiteful. Roomy armchairs, sofas, studio couches—all these are unsafe. And as to beds, no girl sincere about resisting will ever enter a room containing one. If you must occupy a couch, remain upright.

In recent years there has been a trend towards floor-sitting. It is casual, bohemian, and seemingly innocent. Shun the floor as you would the bed! Actually, the only difference between the two is that a floor offers a larger surface and is less comfortable.

Some girls make the mistake of thinking they are safe when standing. On the contrary, to stand is to invite trouble. A standing object is approachable from any angle. Next to lying down, standing up is the most vulnerable position you can assume.

The smartest move on entering a room is to seize upon any small straight chair (preferably armless) and sit on it quickly. As long as you can maintain your position on such a chair, you are not in any immediate danger.

Wherever you may be, indoors or out—try to keep moving. Avoid the horizontal and the vertical. Stay away from corners. Do not lean against tables, trees, or walls. The expression "one's back to the wall," which is used to

 I know one secretary whose boss always took her with him to the safe-deposit vault to check his securities, with disastrous results.

denote a completely defenceless position, is in itself a fair warning.

If all these precautions seem to leave you up in the air, remember it is not an easy matter to circumvent Nature. If you truly want to resist, and are willing to go to the trouble and expense of creating an ideal setting, I suggest a room such as the one sketched below.

Observe—there are no walls, only windows. The room is brilliantly lighted with spotlights and is circular in form, thereby eliminating corners. The windows have neither curtains, drapes, nor blinds. All the chairs are small and straight, the tables are fragile, floral decorations are large and obtrusive, and the interesting spikework that covers the floor offers ample room for walking but forbids sitting or reclining.

Should you be unable to avoid a dangerous location, you will be starting out at a disadvantage. But that is no reason to throw up your hands and surrender. Divert him, discourage him, dissuade him. You still have a fighting chance.

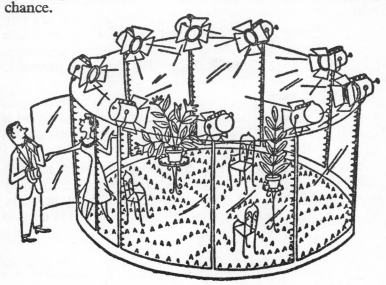

## *Evasions*

The ordinary, everyday activities are the most effective:

### EATING

Nibble constantly. Keep one jump ahead of him. Each time he is about to kiss you, pop something into your mouth, a chocolate, a cough lozenge, anything.

### DRINKING

Hold a glass filled with liquid. Lift it frequently to your lips, and at times wave it gracefully in his direction. This will make him keep a safe distance, for no man wants something spilled on his clothes or in his ear.

### SMOKING

If you are sufficiently careless about the way you handle a lighted cigarette, it becomes an excellent weapon of defence. Just the smallest burn, or even a singe, will make him disinclined to clutch you in his arms a second time.

## FIDDLING

A line of defence which works best in your own home is that of keeping busy. Whenever he is about to score a point, get up and do something. Be warm and even affectionate towards him, but empty ashtrays, or bring him some refreshment, or pick up a scrap of paper, or comb your hair, or powder your nose. It is fun to see how many things you can think up to fuss with.

## TALKING

Talk is good. Do not chatter aimlessly, as this will drive him away entirely. Say something that will arrest his attention, and hold his interest—as you would distract a baby with some bright toy when it reaches for an object it should not have. Each time the conversation runs down, and he is about to resume his advances, take his hands in yours, draw a deep breath, and start off with:

When you were a little boy, were you . . . or
Do you believe in equality of the sexes? . . . or
Betty said something odd about you . . . or
Do you know what I thought the first time I saw you?

Eating, Drinking, Smoking, Fiddling, Talking—if you are clever enough to juggle all these evasions at once you can put up an effective barricade and throw a man off his game for hours. Do not take off your hat. Do not take off your shoes. Act sweet and friendly, and appear to be completely unaware that you are thwarting him. Often he will not even realize why he has made no headway. He will blame himself for mishandling the situation, as indeed he should. For a really capable male will take away your cigarette, chocolates, drink, hat, shoes, et cetera, and disregard your conversation.

# THE UNFAIR SEX

## *How To Say No If You Must*

Sometimes despite a carefully selected locale and well-executed evasions, you somehow find yourself encircled, and your only out is a direct verbal rejection.

A light touch is the prime requisite. It is ridiculous to get annoyed with men for trying. If you object to their vulgar advances, you had best stop associating with them. Maintain a sense of balance. Realize Man is your adversary, and that you must fight him, but realize it with a catch in your breath and a little thrill of anticipation, not with anger or resentment.

A man will be much less hurt if he is teased or gently discouraged from carrying out his dishonourable intentions, than he will if you sulk, struggle, or lose your temper. The man who is trying to conquer a woman is engaged in a grave undertaking. And nothing is so irritating in the face of his own problems as a woman who tries to focus attention on hers. Consider how trivial your pride and dignity must seem to a man absorbed in preserving *his* pride and dignity. Preoccupation with your own interests will make him feel you are self-centred and inconsiderate.

Remember, a man considers a rejection a personal affront. In his brutish way he reasons: "This female is apparently normal—she must make love sometime—with someone. What has she got against me?" And you will never hear from him again.

But if you treat the situation lightly he will think you do not know you are in danger—and he will admire you for such foolish femininity. And if you say No with a smile, he will believe you do not mean it. Again and again he will return to you, happy in the thought that you are constantly on the verge of giving in.

Sprinkle the combat with small favours and soft words. This will lessen the bitterness of the struggle and charm your foe into liking you regardless of who the victor may be. Above all, never let him become depressed. Do not let him see you distrust him. Keep smiling. Smile with your eyes, or dimple at him if you have dimples, or chuckle or giggle—and once in a while you may laugh outright—especially if you have pretty teeth, or if someone is tickling you—which someone may very well be doing.* But be extremely careful that your gaiety is the right sort. He must never suspect you are laughing *at* him, even when he is making a fool of himself.

Your objections should seem carefree and artless, an effect one must be very artful to achieve. Here is a little experiment which you might make in front of a mirror:

First say the following words with a scowling face and an angry voice:

No.

Stop it—I'm serious.

I'll scream.

If you don't stop I'm going home.

Oh! Now I'm angry.

Please!

Didn't you seem mean and stubborn? These are not qualities that will endear you to a man. *Now*—say the same words, but say them with a charming smile, and in a gently chiding tone. Or seriously, but interspersed with little giggles. Or with reproving but loving looks, as if you were speaking to a naughty puppy.

There—you have said the *very same words*—but how delightful you looked and sounded!

It may be argued that this is dangerous, as it makes you doubly desirable, and the man will want you even more. Don't you believe it! He will want you neither more nor less. But the *How* and *Why* he wants you will be different.

---

In passing, I should like to say a brief word against Tickling. This activity is in the same class as Wrestling. Each is a means of wearing down resistance, and while it seems like good clean fun, it is actually a Technique.

He will be determined to have the mean and stubborn girl out of spite. But the smiling, charming girl he will insist on having because she is so adorable. For Which Reason Would You Rather Be Had?

Any tyro can bluntly reject a man and thereby lose him. It takes study and practice to acquire the agility to send him away happy though rejected. An accomplished girl can do this. She can hold him off, yet bring him back for another try. And bringing him back is essential. For unless a man is a complete boor (and sometimes, alas, even if he is) you will want to hold on to him for purposes of entertainment or advancement, or as a marital prospect. When you can, *without offending*, deny him the pleasures he so understandably desires, you will know you have mastered the delicate technique of passive resistance.

## CHAPTER ELEVEN

# The Pangs and Pains
# of Giving

*"The sins they do by two and two, they must pay for one by one."*
—KIPLING

THERE is always a percentage in every group—the reckless, the curious, the stupid, the perverse, and those who are just plain naughty—who will disregard warnings and hasten to "see for themselves."

In most cases the would-be sinner contemplates the future with unbecoming levity. She starts out with the fatuous assumption that she can give herself easily, naturally, like rolling off a log. Somewhere in the back of her head is the childish belief that she will have fun, that pleasure and happiness are to be found easily in that which is forbidden. Common sense should tell her she is mistaken.

If what she assumes were true, the word would soon pass from mouth to mouth, and no amount of laws, social rules, sermons and punishments could stem the rush of the entire female population toward this particular misdeed. For happiness is at a great premium, and no one would hesitate to smash a few laws to attain it, particularly laws which have no teeth in them.

121

## THE UNFAIR SEX

It is interesting to examine the stringent penalties that were imposed on wayward females in Puritan New England of the seventeenth and eighteenth centuries. I doubt that the girls of our present, rather effete society would exhibit the same hardihood as the pioneer woman did, in defying the restrictions of those earlier days. The records indicate that severe and public chastisement did little to deter the wilfulness of Puritan maidens. The incidence of illegitimate children* in that era was so high that in time it became necessary to accept a girl's first illegitimate child as a matter of course, and no disgrace accrued to the wrongdoer unless she gave proof of a second indiscretion.

Parents try to frighten today's girls with threats of *Disgrace*, enforced *Spinsterhood*, and unwilling *Motherhood*. It

And obviously, the number of bastards on record is not an accurate index to the number of irregularities that occurred, since the ratio of misdeed to offspring is never constant.

is unfortunate that these threats are so patently false. A girl who can read, a girl who has any intelligence at all realizes that they present no more actual danger than the laws referred to above.

She knows there need be no *Disgrace*. The very nature of the deed lends itself to the utmost secrecy, and the employment of ordinary discretion would keep the matter private. Since there is no outward evidence* of her dereliction, it can be discovered only if she is unable to resist boasting. There is no instance on record of a girl being fired from her job, or shunned by her friends because she bestowed her favours on a man. (I speak, naturally, of the nice girl who conducts her affairs like a lady. One who is crude and vulgar will be ostracized even if she is a virgin.)

A well-bred girl realizes that what is most important is to avoid the appearance of wrong-doing—that she will suffer Disgrace only through her own carelessness. Or because of treachery on the part of the man. But there is little to fear from the latter source, since everyone knows that men are notorious liars, quick to brag of conquests they have never made. Consequently, a sneering feminine denial will carry as much weight as a leering masculine boast. And every sensible girl will be quick to give the lie to such a dastardly accusation, even when it is true.

As to *Spinsterhood*, available records reveal that practically all old maids are virgins, which would indicate that only a minute percentage of our erring girls are punished by enforced Spinsterhood. There is little one can add to

---

There are a few old wives' tales to the contrary. My own mother told me there is a light in a girl's eyes which is extinguished immediately pursuant to the loss of virginity. I dutifully believed that all the world could see this tell-tale signal, although I myself was never able to discern the absence or presence of a virginal radiance in anyone's eye.

this mute testimonial, except to say it is lamentable that virtue is not better rewarded.

Lastly, there is the threat of involuntary *Motherhood*. Due to modern scientific developments, illegitimate children are a rarity, the illegitimacy rate being lower for this century than any one preceding it. It is true, there are a few unfortunates every year, but these girls are the kind who, if they did not get into this sort of difficulty, would fall out of a window, or be hit by a car, or suffer some other mishap. They are accident prone.

\*　　\*　　\*

No—it is foolish to think these bogeymen can be used to frighten little girls into good behaviour. But the Truth about Giving—the unvarnished, unglamourized, dehydrated Truth—may carry some weight.

I omit all the moral and ethical arguments supporting a State of Virtue as defined by our Society. And to search for the pure meaning of so-called sin as it appears when held up to a clear light and examined without the distorting shadows cast by our morals and mores—this is not our problem. What I give you here is an analysis of the practical, personal disadvantages of Giving as determined by the pattern of life in this time and place:

### *Failure*

NOT EVERY GIRL WHO GIVES HERSELF IS SO FORTUNATE AS TO HAVE THE DONATION RESULT IN AN AFFAIR.

And it is precisely this fact which produces the most profound despair.

To the beginner, contemplating her maiden voyage, I particularly address the following, though it applies as well to the girl who is making her third, fifth or seventeenth trip.

It is likely that if you have decided to bestow your favours on a man, you have selected someone you like or love. In other words, your emotions are involved, and if they are not at the outset, they will be before the finish—of this you can be sure. Women are unable to divorce tender emotions from sex. A man, *no matter how well he may conceal his attitude*, takes the matter lightly without embarrassing his heart. He attaches no more consideration to it than to eating his dinner, pleased if it is well cooked,

disappointed if it is not. You are embarking on what you consider an extraordinary undertaking—accompanied by a partner who thinks it is a trivial incident.

I also assume that you do not enter into this intimate relationship with the thought that it is to be of a fleeting nature. Rather do you look upon it as the beginning of a wonderful association; you expect that you will mean very much more to him now; that you will have a strong hold on him; and that the future promises all the romantic pleasures an innocent girl imagines she has the right to expect from an affair. In other words, your dreams are hooked on to this man.

But alas! It is a man's way with a maid to give no more thought to the future than a grasshopper. He is perfectly capable of dropping you immediately after he has had his way with you. And this he does, with a frequency that is disheartening. Could anything make you feel more dejected, more devastated, more exasperated?

It is possible the man may invite you to give yourself a second or third time and *then* drop you. Personally, I have found it less heartbreaking to be dropped after the one tryst, for while that carries the shock of a decapitation, there is some mercy in a quick and sudden ending. Far more anguish is entailed in a finis that comes after several instalments, because the expectations of the female grow during even a short period of time, and the wound therefore goes deeper. But in either event it is a setback which shakes a girl's ego to its very foundations, sometimes leaving a scar that even marriage, or two or three marriages, cannot heal.

THIS RUDE DESERTION IS THE FIRST AND MOST FREQUENT OF THE SHATTERING CONSEQUENCES OF GIVING.

Despite the fact that seventy-two per cent of all seductions wind up in this sad manner, it is possible that you will be more fortunate than the majority of your sisters, and your misstep may be the beginning of an affair that will at least run its full course.

## *Disappointment*

At the outset you have no way of knowing whether you are in the seventy-two per cent class or in with the lucky twenty-eight per centers. For—steady beau or fly-by-nighter—you get the same nasty jolt the next morning. You expect an early phone call. You expect some indication, either by words, deed, or token, that something momentous has happened. You expect him to feel the same heart-stirring excitement that you do. But there is no phone call, no box of flowers—nothing. Just an outrageous silence.

For those in the seventy-two per cent group, this silence will of course be unbroken. If, on the other hand, this is to be the dawn of an affair, the wretch will phone or write after an endless interval of twenty-four hours, or three days, or even a week—cheerfully unaware that he has been remiss.

The most sincere lover in the world can be guilty of just such callous behaviour. There is a great, male blind spot concerning this, and if only men could be made to understand how essential are the morning-after attentions, there would be a lot less grief in the world. Even a diamond bracelet the following week (and who is so lucky as to get a diamond bracelet?) can barely make up for the suffering caused by neglect on that following morning.

However, because it is not nice to start bickering so early in a love affair, you must overlook his inattentiveness and nurse your hurt privately. Observe how quickly and inevitably unhappiness follows your slip from grace.

In rapid succession you realize a number of unpleasant facts:

1.   The new set-up has brought him no closer to you emotionally.

2.   He feels neither grateful nor obligated.

3.   Instead of being more attentive, he is less so, following the age-old precept that there is no point in chasing a bus after you have caught it.

This, then, is the initial stage of an affair—not at all like the romantic delirium you expected. But—you carry on, hoping to find somewhere some sweet reward for your folly. Instead, you discover that your happiness is restricted by a number of inescapable factors.

## Secrecy

In this bold adventure, you are obliged to maintain a careful screen of secrecy. You cannot introduce your lover to your family and friends and say that he belongs to you. You cannot even afford to be seen together constantly. For if you are not betrothed and can give no indication that marriage is in the offing, how can you explain the relationship between you?

After all, a sizeable portion of a woman's pleasure in a man is derived from letting the world know he is hers. Keeping him hidden is like owning a mink coat which you may never take out of your bedroom. It is necessary to have the envy of others in order to enjoy true happiness.

## Compromise

An affair is always a compromise—a settling for what you can get in place of that which you want—i.e., marriage. And it would seem that in making such a compromise, the least one might expect in compensation is a completely satisfactory partner. But the perfect partner in a liaison is as difficult to find as the perfect partner in marriage. As in a game of cards, you may be dealt one poor hand after another, and unless you want to turn your back on the game, you must make the best of it.

Waiting stubbornly for perfection often resolves itself into a negation of all action. Therefore, one not only accepts an affair instead of marriage, one also frequently settles for a second- or third-choice man to have it with.

And why can you not have marriage with this first-, second- or third-choice partner? Usually, it is because he Does Not Love You, or he is Financially Handicapped, or he is Already Married.

There is little need to expand on the Pain of Not Being Loved. It is the nature of a female to expect love from a man to whom she gives herself. If you are at all sensitive, you will continually smart under the insult of his moderate affection.

If, on the other hand, he does love you but Cannot Afford Marriage, you wonder—will he ever improve his status? And when he does, will he still want you? You suspect you are losing valuable time and letting other prospects slip through your fingers.

Most distressing of all is the man who is Already Married. The complexities and problems of such an affair are too numerous for discussion here. They will be taken up in a special chapter.

## *Humiliation*

By all that you have seen, read and learned since you were a little girl, you are conditioned for wifehood. In exchange for giving yourself, it seems like simple justice to receive the lifetime benefits of marriage, to be protected by law, respected by society, and enabled to dictate your desires and needs to a husband. It is contrary to all your instincts to give to a man who is under no obligation to you. He is the conqueror—you are the conquered. You cannot help but find such a reversal of custom insufferable. You have made a poor bargain, and no woman who makes a poor bargain can ever really be happy with it.

## *Impermanence*

It seems unfair that an amour, which lacks the benefits of marriage, should nevertheless be burdened with the same ills. But such is the case. The high spirits, the exuberance, the fireworks of the initial period (which corresponds to the honeymoon in marriage) peter out in the natural course of events. The anti-climactic let-down —the flatness which normally ensues—is extremely trying. You are deprived of the opiates of cooking and cleaning and marketing, of bearing and rearing children, of visiting and being visited by his friends and relations, and all the other blessings which help so much to alleviate the boredom of marriage, and make for a full empty life.

Moreover, since in a marriage one expects little more than comfort and convenience, the disillusionment of the post-honeymoon period is taken philosophically. But for the couple who is living in sin, what is left for them when the *raison d'etre*, the excitement of a new love, is gone? Nothing.

There is a temptation to sever the relationship at this point. It is usually all so very simple—just a quiet chat, a handshake, and a tear or two. Occasionally, of course, there may be a suicide or a homicide. But there is none of the expense and nuisance which makes divorce so unattractive. Furthermore, the termination of an affair gives the participants a beautiful, clean feeling of Virtue Revisited, whereas a divorce carries with it a sense of failure.

The ease with which an affair can be ended is one of its most unfortunate aspects. Having transgressed once, no matter how unsuccessfully, a woman has less resistance to making the mistake a second time. She may, indeed, become addicted to this sort of thing and be tempted to spend her life hopping from one unsanctified honeymoon to another. This is comparable to the habit of selecting only the choice bonbons from a box and throwing away the remainder. Such wastefulness and self-indulgence indicate a sad lack of character, and one instinctively disapproves of the woman who takes the best of a man and can find no use for the rest of him.

There are several directions an affair can take—none of them entirely satisfactory:

1. As your relationship progresses, you become accustomed to his masculine ways, his casual attitude, his inattentiveness, etc., and with true feminine tenderness you come to depend on him and to need him. And you are miserable. You feel insecure and unloved and frustrated, because this dear man insists on retaining the right to abandon you at whim.

No matter how happy you make him, he will some day wander away*—leaving you sorry and forlorn among the débris of your dreams.

2. By careful handling, you may so endear yourself to him that he will eventually marry you. For the sake of accuracy, I must report that in the twenty-eight per cent group this is a not uncommon occurrence.

3. Should he decide to marry you, and you—not fancying him as a husband—refuse, you will find it impossible to continue with him. There will be a disagreeable finale, in which he will heap on you all the angry accusations which are traditionally made by a "wronged woman."

He seeks not an improvement but a change. In a neat, civilized world there are few avenues of adventure open to a man. When he gets tired of living in the same city, working at the same job, following always the same routine—when he longs to go off to some far corner of the world—he does nothing about it. Common sense forbids, and he can satisfy his restless spirit only by acquiring a new woman.

4. If you are proud, you will be unable to endure an affair which falls short of your romantic dreams in so many ways, and you will call an abrupt halt. (This is puzzling to a man and gives rise to one of those masculine slogans—"Can't ever understand a woman.") You will have salvaged some of your pride by dismissing him, but you will be forever tormented by the suspicion that he got the better of you.

5. You may have the stamina to weather the disillusioning early stages of an affair, but find yourself getting squeamish after the shakedown period. You hate sneaking about, you have an oppressive sense of guilt, you remember all the lessons of your childhood, you fear hell and damnation, and you decide that after all you have made a bad mistake. But miserable and cold, you hang on, hoping that he will marry you and provide the consolation of retroactive sanctification.

Down so many ill-starred paths can an unlicensed alliance carry you. And there are others, too personal, too painful, or too sensational for public discussion. Is it not obvious that a girl has little chance of finding happiness in the badlands? Even if there should be moments cf ecstasy (and of this there is no guarantee) they are hardly compensation for all the aggravation you suffer when you live outside the law.

## CHAPTER TWELVE

# Why Didn't I Hear from Him Again?

THIS plaintive cry has echoed in the heart of every woman at some time or other in her life. Even the most glamorous, the most sought-after, are faced with the enigma of the man who seems captivated, and yet never calls again.

There are two important types from whom one does not hear again.

Type I takes you and then drops you.

Type II takes your phone number and never uses it.

Why? Why do such awful things happen? And what can be done to prevent them? Let us first examine the causes, which are the same in either case.

Ask yourself if you committed any of the following errors:

> Did you talk too much?
> Did you talk about marriage?
> Did you make him spend too much?
> Did you make him feel inferior?

133

Did you boast?
Did you laugh too loud?
Did you accept him too eagerly?
Did you refuse him too definitely?

On the other hand, your failure may have nothing to do with you at all—not with your appearance, your personality, your behaviour, nor with the fact that you did or did not give yourself.

Often you have done nothing wrong, but are merely the victim of circumstances beyond your control. The most important fact for you to realize is:

 *A man does not spring into existence at the moment you meet him.*

He has already lived a whole life—the more attractive and interesting the man, the more full and interesting a life. He has not been holding himself in readiness for the day you accidentally cross his path, but has already formed ties, obligations and interests. It is very possible he is—

## Not in the Market

He may have a sweetheart who is entirely satisfactory, and his attentions to you are based on the fact that:

1.   She is away for a few weeks and he requires feminine companionship, or

2.   They have had a little quarrel, or

3.   He is restless and seeking a temporary diversion, or

4.   He wants an extra just in case—or just because.

There is slight chance of your appropriating him permanently in any of the above cases—except possibly Number Four. Remember—his sweetheart knows his tastes and his moods, his weaknesses and his idiosyncrasies—and in one or two tries you cannot hope to catch up with her. Few men will disturb a smoothly running alliance to start a new one.

## *Shopping*

A man may be fresh out of girls and looking for a replacement. Still, he is not likely to make an on-the-spot decision about a new one, any more than he would move into the first house he looked at. He wants to think you over. Are you really as cute as he said you were? Did you get a little boring the last half hour? Aren't you a bit too tall or too thin for him? Was it a long trip home after he left you? Are you worth the trouble?

While he is absorbed with these questions, he meets a

girl who has a forty-two-foot sloop or hair that smells like his mother's, and he will fall madly in love with her and never call you again.

There is also the possibility that you have met a shopper who is not so self-confident as he seems. Perhaps he has made boastful claims for himself and fears he can never live up to them. Or he may feel he has already given evidence of his inadequacy. For him it will be a relief never to have to face you again.

Or—he may be discouraged by your assets. Are you too brainy for him? Too well dressed? Are you so popular he will have to struggle to hold on to you? If so, he may pass you up in favour of a plain girl with just enough brains to invest her savings in a pair of season tickets to the Arsenal.

As every shop assistant knows, it is twice as difficult to make a sale if the shopper has a friend along. A wise girl avoids meeting a man's friends or family until after she has got a toehold on his affections. When old and trusted associates attack a new sweetheart, the newcomer has little chance of survival.

### The Fly-by-Nighter

This man has no sweetheart and is not looking for one, for he is incapable of making a woman happy. But driven by the wish to appear every inch a man, he plods bravely through a series of fleeting incidents, relying on a string of deserted females to stand silent witness to his virility.

A variant of the Fly-by-Nighter is the Don Juan.* He has been hurt by a woman, or by several women, and

Don Juan was deserted in childhood by his mother, and spent his life making women love him only so that he might abandon and hurt them as he had been abandoned and hurt.

triggered by his determination to have revenge, he has more than the usual amount of masculine drive. As a rule, he is quite attractive. (The unattractive ones are obliged to swallow their hurt.) So charming is he, so eager, so adroit, that you rarely recognize him for what he is until after he has delivered the blow.

## Stalemate

There is one kind of man who, though he gives outward evidence of being captured by your charms, is not really interested. He is not interested in girls at all. But he wishes to give the impression that he is, and thus gain the approval of those who would otherwise censure him. He is a polite and civilized individual who is trying to conform to a social code which forbids deviations and which refuses to acknowledge the existence of such deviations. Separated only by a hairline from the Don Juan, he is somehow more easily forgiven.

So varied and understandable are the reasons behind the sudden withdrawal of a man's attentions. Knowing them, you need not let an abandonment depress you or shake your self-confidence. Accept each one philosophically. More important, try to anticipate the unpleasant event and forestall it.

## In Defence

AGAINST TYPE ONE

Type One is the man who seduces, then drops you. You get that dreadful left-over feeling the minute he says good-bye. You search about for some sign of hope, but even the furniture looks depressed. The telephone has a strangely dead look, as if it will never ring again—and there you stand, with the vague and sheepish feeling that you have been had. And indeed you have.

There is one infallible way to avoid this bleakest of tragedies—Never Give Yourself.

If for any reason you are unable to follow this rule, there is another, but less dependable one—Never Give Yourself in Haste. Allow a reasonable amount of time to elapse between the moment of meeting and the moment of surrender. Impose on yourself an Enforced Waiting Period, and no matter how much you feel tempted, do not let yourself give in before the time is up.* This will do you good in more ways than one. A man who is sincere about wanting you is usually willing to put a little time and energy into the pursuit. The others, the undesirables, you can shake off easily, like shaking rotten apples off a bough.

For, generally speaking, the man whose intentions are of the worst has little patience. The philanderer who has a sweetheart—the important man looking for recreation—the traveller in town for a limited stay—the Fly-by-Nighter—each one seeks a momentary diversion and is unwilling to expend much effort. Dilly-dallying on your part will result in his dropping you *before* instead of immediately *after* he has had you. Which is like taking a small bitter pill to ward off a dread affliction.

As to the fellow who is shopping and really wants a girl —the fact that you are too readily accessible often counts against you. Secretly or openly, every male rejoices in the belief that he has overcome a woman by virtue of his superior wit or weight. The chase is as exciting as the capture, and he will not forgive you if you run to meet him halfway. Furthermore, if you give yourself casually, you

 I trust that you will remember the lessons on how to resist a man, and that your refusals will always hold the sweet hint of a future acceptance.

must expect the man to take you casually, and leave you in the same spirit. It is human to place little value on that which is given away freely.

If, during the Enforced Waiting Period, you find your resolve slipping, strength can be found in repeated recitation of the sixteen Joys of Man, and in serious meditation on the Joys and Rewards of Refusing. Having successfully weathered this difficult period, you may proceed with the feeling that you have taken all reasonable precautions. But men being such unpredictable creatures, the outcome of course is in the lap of the gods.

## AGAINST TYPE TWO

While harmless compared to Type One, Type Two is every bit as exasperating, and much more difficult to recognize.

Whatever the circumstances of your meeting may be, this man singles you out for attention. He flatters you, confides in you, indicates in every way that he is smitten. If possible, he escorts you home. He seems reluctant to leave and pretends he is eager to see you again. *But*—he does not make a date. He does not say, "Are you free tomorrow night?—or the night after?—or any night?" Instead, he takes out a little crumpled scrap of paper and says, "What's your phone number? I'll give you a ring." And you never never hear from him again.

Frankly, there is little you can do to protect yourself against this kind of disappointment. However, there is one device which I have employed with a fair degree of success:

 *When he asks for your phone number, do not give it to him.*

Instead, quickly say: "Let me have *your* phone number,

and I'll call you as soon as I'm free." Or, "I never get my messages. Better let me phone you."

This unexpected turning of the tables will certainly surprise him, and may even confuse him, which is always desirable.

If he hedges and insists on having yours, give him a wrong number and forget him. Any man who will not give a girl his number is suspect. But in all likelihood, he will be caught off balance and give you his number without argument.

Now you are protected! He does not have your number —how can he disappoint you, even if he wants to? And if he intends to forget you, he cannot—you have *his* number!

Often a man needs a little help in making up his mind, and the sound of your voice may jog him into action. Most people find it difficult to say No. Have you not made contributions or bought magazines only because you were too soft-hearted to decline? Why should this principle not operate in *your* favour? The man will be more or less obliged to see you if you call, and one can afford to leave no stone unturned in a world so sparsely supplied with attractive men.

Of course, like most tricks, the Telephone Trick does not always work. He may not remember who you are. *Do not remind him.* Hang up! And throw away his number. You must use good judgment in determining whether the man is pleased or annoyed to hear from you.

If he remembers you but does not make a date—throw away his number. He has had two chances, and no unattached man is so busy he cannot spare a few hours for someone he really wants to see. He has to eat dinner, hasn't he? Why won't he eat it with you?

Oh well—the success or failure of your phone calls is relatively unimportant. The real advantage of not giving out your number is that you do away with that horrible period of watching the telephone. No longer need you spend two or three weeks waiting and wondering:

# WHY DIDN'T I HEAR FROM HIM AGAIN?

Maybe he lost the little scrap of paper.
Maybe my phone is out of order.
Maybe he called while I was out.
Maybe he's sick.
Maybe he's shy.
Maybe he's dead.

No more of that! Now you will *know* if he is sick and forgetful—or alive and unwilling!

It gives you a lovely feeling of superiority to have a man's number when he does not have yours. The decision rests with you. You can take your time and decide if *you* really want to see *him*. You might wait two weeks, three, four—just to tease him. Or you might *never* phone him, and let a *man* know how it feels to wait and wait for a call that never comes.

## CHAPTER THIRTEEN

# The Joys and Rewards
# of Refusing

*"Take hand and part with laughter; touch lips and part with tears."*
—SWINBURNE

OFTEN a woman achieves more real happiness, that is to say gratification of the Ego, in the rejection of one man than in the acceptance of a dozen. Naturally, this is true only if the rejected man is a desirable one. No particular honour attaches to a woman who rejects a lemon—a man whom no one would have except in marriage. Assuming, therefore, that the reject is an acceptable male, there is much to be gained, i.e.,

The glory of Victory. You have withstood the assault and bested the foe.

The warm glow of Relief. This is one man who will never have you at a disadvantage.

An enormous sense of Power. You know that you have the ability to attract a desirable man and the strength to deny yourself to him.

And—there is also the delight of being quite Extravagant. You have tossed aside a man just as if there were dozens more waiting for you.

Added to these immediate blessings, there are a number of long-range benefits:

For many days and months, and even years, you will hug to yourself the satisfying memory of how he pleaded, how you refused, what he said, how he looked, how you looked, what he must have thought and felt, how he must still long for you, etc.

The recollection of one rejection can suffice to:

1.  Bolster your ego in those periods when you are without a beau.

2.  Solace you when you are jilted by some other man.

3.  Salve your conscience when it appears you have said Yes too often.

Never will the rejected man lose his appeal. He will remain fresh in your memory, like a charming compliment.

And as time passes, you will endow him with added virtues, for as his value is magnified, so the pleasure of having rejected him will increase.

I know a girl who, in a mad moment of self-glorification, rejected a handsome movie star. Had she accepted him, he inevitably would have disappointed her in some way, and her feeling towards him now would be a bitter one. But having said No, she retains the warmest affection for him, goes to see all his movies, keeps his picture on her dressing-table, and feels a warm surge of pleasure every time she hears his name or sees it in print. And nothing could persuade her that she does not hold a special place in his memory, for she is certain no other woman ever turned him away.

(Not everyone is so fortunate as to have the opportunity of doing things on such a grand scale. But each in her own sphere can achieve proportionate success.)

If the rejected man is one whom you will meet often, your rewards are multiplied. Each time you see him, you will enjoy the conviction that here is a human being who thirsts for you. Should he be without a woman you will think, "Ha! If he cannot have me, he'd rather do without." If he has acquired a wife or a sweetheart, or several sweethearts, you will think, "Poor boy, he is trying to forget me." Towards any woman who grants this man her favours, you will have a smug feeling of superiority. What you rejected, she has accepted.

Another source of gratification is the fact that your triumph over a man need not be kept secret. In fact, it never is. Whereas your capitulation to a most delightful man must be kept discreetly hidden, there is every reason to tell all who will listen—your friends, enemies, relatives, acquaintances, and manicurist—about this wonderful man who tried and tried but failed to shake you. All who hear the tale will be impressed with your virtue, convinced of your popularity, and filled with a determination to go and do likewise. "I'm going to do that the very next time someone asks me," each will say to herself.)

Often this starts a whole rash of rejections—particularly of the man you rejected—since no woman with any pride wants a man who has just been refused.

It is to be hoped you will have too much good sense to boast to other men about your refusal. For out of a peculiar kind of loyalty to their sex, they will resent your publicizing a fellow man's failure. They consider it bad sportsmanship. You must perforce trust to luck that the news will get around from other sources. You will then find yourself very much in demand, for next to stealing a friend's wife or sweetheart, nothing is so appealing to a man as the idea of succeeding where some other fellow has failed.

(Warning—Accept this sudden popularity with the realization that it is built on a dangerous foundation and be very much on guard, or you will find yourself paying Peter for what you did to Paul.)

# THE UNFAIR SEX

Despite the fact that a rejection requires will-power and foresight and self-denial, numbers of women are successful in accomplishing it. Some, after achieving it once, find they can repeat the coup over and over again with increasing ease. The dangers of this practice are so apparent to the whole male race that throughout the pages of literature one can read their condemnation.*

I have set forth in this chapter the realistic down to earth facts, presented from a female point of view. And if I succeed in persuading even *one solitary* reader that there are more genuine delights to be obtained from walking in the path of virtue than in exploring uncharted byways, I shall consider my work well done.

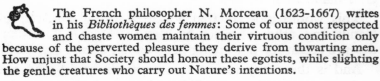

The French philosopher N. Morceau (1623-1667) writes in his *Bibliothèques des femmes*: Some of our most respected and chaste women maintain their virtuous condition only because of the perverted pleasure they derive from thwarting men. How unjust that Society should honour these egotists, while slighting the gentle creatures who carry out Nature's intentions.

## CHAPTER FOURTEEN

# Virtue

WHEN one speaks of virtue in connection with a woman, one does not mean honesty, piety, loyalty, integrity, generosity, or courage. The only important female virtue is Chastity. Yet the universal homage it receives is not always deserved. Too often the female maintains a state of sanctity not because she possesses nobility of character and purity of soul, but merely as a result of chance.

An outstanding example of this is the Biological Variance Factor. The B.V.F., as scientists label it, is a rather complicated way of explaining that not all human beings fit into the same pattern. The needs, the appetites, the desires of some are greater than others, and are determined not by the Devil's promptings, but by the way God made their bodies.

This would indicate that Virtue is often a matter of glands and other vagaries of Nature. Does a girl then deserve credit for not giving in to an urge she never had?

And is there any reason to esteem the maid who has

never been asked? What proof do we have that she could successfully withstand an assault on her virtue? She is chaste only by default.

As to the woman who has both the Urge and the Temptation, but steadfastly denies herself what she wants simply because she is afraid—is it fitting to pay homage to a coward?

Careful investigation reveals an amazing variety of reasons, other than the obvious spiritual ones, which tend to produce Chastity.

A well-known model confessed under pressure that rather than reveal the falsity of her famous curves, she has repulsed all masculine advances. This is not Virtue—this is Vanity.

A pretty career girl I know spends her salary on hairdressers and smart clothes in order to make a stunning appearance on the job. She is forced to economize somewhere, and does so on her underclothes, spending only a bare minimum for replacements. And rather than expose the frayed edges and poor quality of her petticoats, panties, and et ceteras, she retains her virginity. Although this represents Pride rather than Virtue, one cannot but respect such extreme regard for the niceties.

A less depressing example of False Virtue is demonstrated in a story my favourite aunt often tells about herself. It seems that, smitten by the charms of a young man, she lapsed from grace one summer night and committed the error of entering his apartment. Subsequent to crossing the threshold, she rapidly reached the Point of No Return. Some small vestige of awareness remained with her, though, and she became concerned about her dress, a starched organdy creation—the sort of thing that shows every twist and turn. My aunt, knowing she could not venture forth, nor indeed return home, in a dress that bore tell-tale evidence of misdoing, complained that the young man was crushing her gown. He of course advised her to take it off, but this she could not bring herself to do, as she did not know him very well. So preoccupied was she with preserving the crispness of her dress, that the fellow finally became exasperated and permitted her to go home with her Virtue intact. Had the young man owned an iron there would have been a different ending to the story.

Shortly after the above episode, my relative achieved marriage, still in a virginal state. Would you describe Aunt Anna as Chaste—or just Neat?

It is not only Pride, Vanity, Cowardice, or Neatness that can be mistaken for Virtue. Sometimes it is sheer Laziness or Stubbornness. Or Retarded Development. Yet every chaste woman insists that her abstinence be accepted as a sign of immense moral strength.

Despite the many honours heaped on a virtuous woman, there is one vexation ever present for her who has fallen into such a mode of life. As she looks at all the sinful people around her and observes their disgraceful behaviour, she feels a twinge of resentment—even envy. Bad girls seem to have such a good time. And what is more unfair—they apparently do not get punished in this life. (A misconception, of course—but the Virtuous have no way of knowing, never having experienced the Pangs and the Pains.)

However, I am told that good women find a deep inner peace and satisfaction in the knowledge that wrongdoers will be tortured in Eternity. If it were not for this comforting thought, many would find the virtuous life unbearable.

In spite of the difficulties, a state of True Virtue is one we should all strive to attain. In an effort to be helpful, I list here some suggestions:

1. Be serious. If you insist on laughing at everything, you will be unable to appreciate the grave importance of Chastity.

2. Be stingy. If you are bursting with good-will towards all mankind, you are unlikely to know where to draw the line on your Generosity.

3.  Be calculating. Stifle your instincts—they are sure to be bad. An impulsive disposition is guaranteed to get you into mischief.

4.  Be stubborn. Amenability is a trait which makes a girl too susceptible to suggestion. It is better to have people say, "She is so virtuous" rather than, "She is so agreeable."

5.  Be sceptical. A trusting, friendly girl has little chance of retaining her purity.

6.  Be cynical. Never allow yourself to be carried away by the beauty of a June night or a new man. Remember, there is no prettier sight than a marriage certificate.

# VIRTUE

7. Be indifferent. If you are naturally drawn to men, it is possible you were not cut out for the Virtuous Life. You must be able to look upon man with calm disinterest.

In short, it is necessary to be serious, stingy, calculating, stubborn, sceptical, cynical, and indifferent to men.

And the rewards?

 *Virtue Is Its Own Reward*

CHAPTER FIFTEEN

# Never Go to a Man's Flat

IT matters not what harmless purpose entices a girl to do so—by simply crossing a man's threshold, she has made an unspoken promise and forfeits the right to be offended by anything that transpires. This is an unwritten law, a universal convention. Visiting a man in his own camp is tantamount to laying down your arms in surrender. No error in judgment, no tactical blunder has more fatal results than this, which is known as "crossing." Yet there are grown women, so trusting or so foolhardy that, ignoring the implications, they enter the enemy's quarters again and again, believing each time that they will come out on top. Their chances are almost nil.

Man has never been able to contrive a more reliable situation than the *tête-à-tête* under his own roof. Consequently, he will lie, scheme, and stoop to any trick to effect a Crossing. Rarely does he issue a straightforward invitation. Instead he resorts to such double-tongued euphemisms as:

Let's go up to my place, and I'll get you a steak dinner.

I expect an important phone call at nine. Do you mind coming back to the hotel with me?

I think I am going to need my overcoat. We'll have to stop off at my room before we go downtown.

I wish you'd come up and look at my flat. I need some ideas on how to decorate.

Hell! Forgot to feed the dog. Come on home with me. It won't take a minute.

(on the phone) I'm sick in bed. Could you come up and bring me some chicken broth?

I wouldn't think of letting you sit alone in a hotel lobby—it isn't safe! You come upstairs with me while I get my brief-case.

Say, I promised to look in at my friend's flat and water his plants while he's away. Want to come along and see his geraniums?

Why don't you come up and read a book while I shave?

I want you to come up and hear those records.

,, ,, ,, ,, ,, ,, ,, see those prints.

I want you to come up and see the view from my window.

    ,,  ,,  ,,  ,,  ,,  ,,  ,, look at my scrapbook.

These are all subterfuges and lies. Know them by heart. And—

*Do Not Go*

This sounds like a fairly simple rule—one that every girl can remember. Certainly nothing more is required than the ability to say No. Yet many girls have difficulty in articulating the word. And this is understandable in many circumstances.

Suppose a man you meet at a dance or at the beach offers to take you home, and on the way he suggests stopping for a drink at his flat. In this instance only a girl with the spine of a jelly-fish would have trouble delivering a strong, definite No.

But—suppose you are with a man you know well—someone you have had three or four dates with. And suppose he is taking you home after a delightful evening of dinner and the theatre. And suppose he is a nice-clean-cut-young-man who has observed the limits you set on spooning. And suppose he suggests stopping at his flat to pick up a book he knows you want to read. Here, a flat No would be crude. Therefore, suppose you casually say the book can wait till next time. And suppose he then looks at you with frank, friendly eyes and says he wants you to see his place anyhow, and he seems very enthusiastic about the idea.

This is the kind of predicament that requires strength of will and singleness of purpose. You must avoid thinking "He is different," and "The circumstances are special," and "He would never do a thing like that." With a swift reflex action, negative responses must immediately form in your mind and on your lips. Forget the words he uses, forget the man, strip the proposed action down to essentials—Does or Does It Not Mean Crossing?

When you refuse an ostensibly innocent invitation to Cross, your would-be host is always deeply offended by your lack of trust, or shocked by your evil-mindedness. Accept this calmly. It is merely a ruse to trick you into saying something like, "I do *so* trust you," or "I wasn't *thinking* of anything like that." And then where are you? You will be forced to go home with him to prove your sincerity.

It is not necessary to refuse in a stuffy manner. Applying the principles of Passive Resistance, you should lead him to assume you will accept the next time, or maybe the time after that.

If you lack the finesse to hold him off cleverly, it is wiser to give a forthright refusal, and perhaps lose the man, rather than Cross and Lose All. Enter no man's abode, whether it be a tiny room in a boarding-house or a suite in a fine hotel, a basement flat or a chateau, a shack in the woods or a bungalow on the beach.

There are certain traps which the most cautious girl cannot forsee. Consider the invitation to visit his Friend's Flat. So harmless a bid is seldom declined, because the scoundrel fails to mention that the friend is not home. Only after you arrive at the door, to which your escort happens to have the key, is it remembered the friend is out of town. It is pretty awkward to avoid Crossing at this point.

An even more difficult contretemps occurs when the friend is home, welcomes you, gets you settled comfortably, and then unexpectedly departs to keep a previous engagement, leaving you at your escort's mercy. One cannot but suspect duplicity, and yet it is all so smoothly done there is little opportunity for indignation.

Unhappily, if you fall victim to the Friend's Flat decoy,

you are, through no fault of your own, put in the same helpless position as the girl who deliberately or carelessly Crosses. Well—*c'est la vie*. Console yourself with the thought that one cannot live without taking a certain number of chances. This is one of those calculated risks which a girl must face if she associates with men. However, the number of girls thus put upon amounts to a mere handful, compared to those who wilfully enter a man's dwelling.

Once you set foot in the spider's web, the number of ways you can be fooled into yielding is infinite. Any method of intrigue he chooses to use is doubly potent in

this setting. Here he has all the comforts and conveniences of home, whereas you are on strange territory. The very atmosphere is pregnant with suggestive thoughts.

You have but one safeguard—no matter how much he teases, scoffs, pleads, argues or reasons with you, say "NO, I will not go." Say it lightly, banteringly, seductively, or chidingly—be amused, or gently reproachful, or sweetly apologetic. But above all, be firm. And—DO NOT CROSS.

CHAPTER SIXTEEN

# How To Behave
# When You Get There

*"Having agreed to dine with a cannibal, and subsequently finding herself neck-deep in a cauldron of soup, the true philosopher concerns herself only with the nature and amount of the flavouring with which she is being cooked."*—N. FAREWELL

A FAIRLY high percentage of all those asked eventually wind up under the man's roof. It is not enough to say No; you must also mean it. Since the upshot of Crossing is as it is, and since it is a daily mishap, let us consider how one should conduct oneself under the circumstances.

While every measure must be taken to avoid Crossing, once you have Crossed, it is of paramount importance that you do so again and again—over the same threshold. A refined young lady will observe all the rules of good conduct which would cause her host to consider her a desirable guest, thus insuring an agreeable visit and future invitations.

Let us contemplate proper etiquette for:

1. Those who know what they are doing and intend to face the consequences if necessary; and

2. Those who persist in believing they are making an innocent social call.

Consider the first group first: To begin with, do not get

coy at the door. There is ample time to make the routine protestations before you reach his house. By hanging back at the last second, you may attract the attention of neighbours, or a fussy landlady, and get off to a bad start. Make up your mind—if you are going in, go in quickly and quietly.

After you have made your entrance, observe your host's behaviour closely. If he speaks in hushed tones, and keeps the radio tuned low, take your cue from him. Do not raise your voice. If you wish to protest, do so quietly. Do not laugh too loudly. Do not clack about on your high heels. He may have any one of a dozen reasons for not wishing it known that he is entertaining a lady. On the other hand, if he is unrestrained, you may follow suit.

Do not examine his home with a critical eye and then make some hackneyed remark to the effect that it lacks the touch of a woman's hand. Praise the décor even if it reminds you of an old hotel lobby, and exclaim about the tidiness, though you see dust on all the mouldings. He will glow like a bride.

Do not leave lipstick marks on his linen; do not spill powder on his bureau. Remember—there is an off-chance you may win this man in marriage. You want him to think you would be a tidy person to live with.

If you are left alone for any length of time, control your temptation to poke about and examine his belongings. I know of a girl who was unable to resist snooping. She lifted the lid of an ornate box that rested on a dresser and was promptly rewarded by a loud burst of music. Without pausing to examine the contents of this musical box, she slammed it shut, but—too late—her host had heard the music and hurried back to the bedroom. So embarrassed was she that she could barely wait for her visit to come to an end.

Another girl peeked into her host's desk and glanced through his date pad, his mail, and his cheque book. She discovered the name of another girl in all three, and this annoyed her so much that it ruined what might otherwise have been a delightful evening.

When you are ready to depart, gather up all your belongings carefully. Some girls think it is cute to leave a memento, like a handkerchief, or a hair ornament, or a garter. Do Not Do It. You may embarrass your host most grievously should your souvenir be discovered by the next guest. Of course, if you suspect he has a sweetheart, you may hope to precipitate a quarrel which will result in a rift which will make him yours alone. If you think it worth while, there are a number of ways to leave tell-tale signs of your visit, not the least of which is to bite your host.

Do not wear out your welcome. Watch the clock more diligently than Cinderella and be sure to leave before the man becomes tired. Unless he is a beast, he will take you home anyhow—but he will resent it, and his opinion of you will be coloured by the memory of that weary, anti-climactic journey.

Do not allow yourself to be carried away by the occasion. If you forget about such matters as the time and the place, you may suddenly discover it is morning. And since Crossing is often done on the spur of the moment, you may be unprepared to face the light of a new day. Many girls are not fit to be seen after a night spent without hair curlers. Others need the benefit of all the little jars and tubes on their dressing-tables. But even if your hair curls naturally and your complexion is divine, you may not be properly dressed. It is most uncomfortable to go home in evening clothes, for instance, at nine or ten in the morning.

A dear friend of mine had a singularly unfortunate experience some years ago. She had been playing tennis in the late afternoon. Her opponent was an attractive man, with whom she had played many times, and she therefore did not hesitate to accept when he invited her to dinner. Wearing sneakers and tennis clothes, and carrying her racquet, she walked blithely into his kitchen . . .

# HOW TO BEHAVE WHEN YOU GET THERE

The next morning, she awoke to find that—one, her host had gone off to his office, leaving a little note that said she slept so prettily he did not want to wake her; and two, it was raining very hard. Only after the door to the apartment had locked behind her, did she discover she could not get a taxi. And so, amid the stares and smiles of the

hordes of people hurrying to their jobs on this rain-drenched Monday morning, she was obliged, as in a bad dream, to walk to the underground and travel home in her little white tennis shorts, racquet in hand.

This episode affected my friend so strongly that she gave up tennis.

There are other unfortunate complications, too many and too varied to be described here, which could result

F                                             161

from overstaying your visit. The well-disciplined girl will make it a rule always to go home early.

All the foregoing is based on the assumption that when you Crossed you knew what you were doing. Now let us consider proper etiquette for the naïve Crosser.

You have been warned—you have been briefed—you have only yourself to blame. Promise yourself you will not let it happen again. That is a nice thought for the future.

For the immediate present:

Do not be a poor loser.

Do not blame the man for your mistake.

Do not cry.

Do not make a scene.

Do not castigate yourself in his presence. Wait till you get home.

All the rules described in this chapter for your more worldly sister should also be observed by you. It is bad enough to be taken, but how much worse to be taken and then dropped. Earn, by your good behaviour, the compliment of subsequent invitations.

And once you have Crossed make up your mind: When the worst happens, you have got to make the best of it. Say as Kipling did, "I have had a jolly good lesson, and it serves me jolly well right!"

## CHAPTER SEVENTEEN

# How To Be Made Love To

So that there will be no confusion, let us come to an understanding about the word "flirting." As used in this chapter, "flirting" (sometimes referred to as "making love") describes the pleasant occupation of kissing, embracing, fondling, caressing, et cetera—*without giving*.

The idea behind flirting goes deeper than the mere gratification of idle personal pleasure.

 *Flirting is the royal road to matrimony.*

It is the means by which you can so possess a man that he will crave more and more of you—and, in fact, all of you—which, of course, you are much too clever to give,*

By coincidence, all the advice offered in this chapter can be utilized also by the girl who insists on committing the error of giving. She need only substitute mentally the word "give" wherever she reads "flirt" or "make love," and she will have a practical guide to help her in her impractical behaviour.

except in exchange for a wedding ring. And this, if you tantalize him properly, he will be obliged to offer.

(Be warned, however, that you always run the risk of losing a man with these tactics, since men are notoriously bad sports and cannot bear to feel they have been tricked or bested. But do not let them shame you into submission with their contempt for unconsummated flirting. The alternative they offer is just as reprehensible.)

During an Initial Flirting Session it is well to exhibit a certain amount of coyness. Give subtle encouragement—but do not be forward. Be feminine, delicate in your speech and posture, gracious about what you give and silent about what you hope to gain. Cloak your eagerness with false modesty. Without behaving as if you have never flirted before, you can nevertheless create the illusion that it is a rare occurrence—something special, reserved for special people and special occasions. This is not only becoming to you—it is also flattering to the man's ego.

A decent interval should be allowed before parting, if only from a standpoint of good manners. Your attitude at this time should be a trifle reserved. Do not appear eager or anxious. *Do not* be possessive. More important, make it difficult for *him* to be possessive. Make sure you are the one to suggest saying goodnight. Do not wait until he says it—it will give you a "left" feeling, and you will wonder, "Was he getting bored?" or "Is he tired of me already?" Rather put *him* in the position of asking these questions.

Each time you see him, conduct yourself with the same grace and caution you displayed the first time—omitting only the coy preliminaries, since once you have flirted with a man, it is difficult to continue a pretence of reluctance without seeming insincere. To be regarded as a good flirting partner, a girl cannot remain coy throughout.

164

## HOW TO BE MADE LOVE TO

Restraint is an admirable feminine attribute, but you should not try to conceal the fact that you like the way he flirts. On the contrary, *be enthusiastic*. No one rule is as important as this. You can make the most ordinary man feel that his kisses are the best in the world. He will be deeply moved by your appreciation and later he will wonder what it was that made flirting with you so unusually gratifying.

A bit of play-acting enters into all love-making. Never give or accept a kiss as nonchalantly as if it were an olive. If you do, you will spoil the game.

Do Not Exhaust the Man physically before you get around to flirting. Do not play two hours of tennis with him, or take him on a long hike, or dance him around until he is limp. No! Keep him fresh and rested. Most men are like hot-house flowers. They wilt easily.

Be lovely. Every woman can seem beautiful when she is being made love to. If your physical charms cannot bear close scrutiny, operate under dim lights. Then you can create the illusion of beauty merely by your manner. As Ovid said, "Darkness makes any woman fair." Smell sweet. Speak gently. Wear materials that are soft to the touch. Above all—*feel* adorable.

Your Mental Attitude when flirting is important. If you have no confidence in your appearance or personality, do not let him know it. If you are afraid he is too forceful to withstand, or too wonderful for you to hold, conceal your fears. A man is like a horse—at the first sign of weakness, the first hint that you are not sure of yourself, he will become headstrong and unmanageable.

Never say "I love you" to a man unless he asks you to do so. While it is every woman's desire to hear these words, a man is a little afraid of them. They forecast complications—faithfulness, marriage, etc. To him the dearest compliment is, "You are a great lover." This is what he is constantly intent on proving to himself, to women and to other men.

Men can become dreadfully dull after a while. If on some occasions your beau, or his kisses, bore you, do not be alarmed. It is inevitable. Try to conceal the unflattering fact beneath an assumed enthusiasm. If the situation does not improve, and you find that you no longer enjoy him at all, you will know the time has come to drop him.

NOTE:

> It is a ridiculous waste of time and energy
> to flirt with a man you do not enjoy.

If by some great good fortune you become enamoured of each other, it is permissible for you to make a display of

warmth and affection, but do not smother him with either. Return his ardour, but do not press your advantage. Do not be aggressive. Let him be the first to make promises, demands, declarations, or suggestions about the future. With proper handling, what started out as a few evenings of innocent fun, may grow into a wonderful romance, and even possibly—marriage.

Do not expect to perform miracles with this brief outline. While the suggestions made here are applicable to the average male, they may not work with equal success on every one you meet. Some men cannot bear uncertainty, and the surest way to their hearts is to make them feel loved and wanted. Others thrive on indifference and teasing. One can love only a lady, another is captivated exclusively by wantons. Study your adversary. When you come across a man you want, learn as much as you can about his likes and dislikes, his temperament and his needs, and—always Play Your Player.

## CHAPTER EIGHTEEN

# How To Drop a Man
# Without Hurting Him

THIS operation is considered by some women to be as pleasing as that of Refusing. How lovely it is to reach the end and realize you got there first! Whether you have retained your chastity or made the tactical blunder of giving all—in either case, the pleasure is now yours. You are about to circumvent the awful jolt of being dropped by a man.

If he has displeased you and thus provoked your decision to drop him, you will want to proceed according to the chapter on how to take the pleasure out of it for him. But if you wish to get rid of him because he has begun to bore you, or you have found someone else, or you suspect he will never propose—deal with him kindly. After all, he is human, he has shared many pleasant hours with you—and besides, you may want him back some day.

Look your prettiest for the occasion. Apply plenty of his

HOW TO DROP A MAN WITHOUT HURTING HIM

favourite perfume, to make certain he will recall you with pain in years to come whenever he passes a perfume counter. Here is an opportunity to wear all the lipstick and false chignons and padding you wish. They will serve to make you look your most appealing and at the same time act as deterrents to any impulse you may have to weaken under his pleading.

By the same token, wear your loveliest dress—preferably one that crushes easily. You will, then, not be tempted should he try to hold you by sentimental means—like using some familiar old embrace.

It is also wise to select an appropriate setting—like a dance floor, or a restaurant, or a party. These places are filled with people, so that not only is it difficult for him to make a fuss, or try to soften you with kisses—but at the same time you have the added pleasure of playing out your little drama before an audience. Your lovely dress, hair, perfume, et cetera, will be exhibited to many, instead of wasted on one man alone—and a played-out one at that.

Your behaviour should be lovable in the extreme. Allow no callous note to creep into your voice. Make him think he is losing a desirable, adorable girl—not a fickle one. Do not reproach him with any past offence. Say it has all been lovely. Tell him you will remember him as one of the nicest people you ever knew. In other words, send him on his way with a sympathetic smile and a warm handshake.

What reason do you give? Certainly not the truth. If he has begun to bore you, be kind enough to conceal this fact from him. Few things can be more wounding to a man's ego. Tell him instead that your mother thinks you are seeing too much of him.

This sometimes results in an impulsive offer of marriage. In such an event, you may want to reconsider. A man who is too dull for a sweetheart may be completely acceptable as a husband. But if you do not want him on any terms, refuse him with a tear.* He has paid you the compliment supreme, and has added to the pleasures of Dropping that of turning down a proposal!

If you have no mother handy, or are too mature to use her for an excuse, tell him you have fallen in love. If by chance you really have found someone else, do not regale the old one with details of the new one's physical, financial, and mental superiority. Slide over these facts gracefully, stating simply that he has asked you to marry him. *Always* say you are going to marry the new man. It will make the old one happy to think he escaped, and he will remember you with gratitude.

If you have no other prospects, but are nevertheless dropping this man because you have given up hope of

 Please note that this is the *only* occasion for which I recommend tears. And it is most likely that your gratification will be so acute you will have little difficulty in bringing them forth.

winning him, state frankly that you want a husband and a home of your own, and you cannot afford to let him monopolize your time any longer. This, too, has been known to precipitate a proposal. But, obviously, no course of action is guaranteed to succeed, so do not try this unless you are ready to drop him, come what may.

In any event, when you undertake to sever relations with a man, do not permit yourself to be unhappy for him. Such sentimentality is misplaced. The fact that he belongs to the male sex is proof positive that he has deeply wounded, or will one day wound, some or many women. The pain you are inflicting is well earned.

And remember—in any romance which does not result in marriage, one of the two people involved must inevitably get dropped. Be thankful that this time it is not you.

CHAPTER NINETEEN

# How To Take The Pleasure
# Out of It for Him

IT is just and fitting that one should suffer for one's mistakes—but how much nicer it is to make someone else suffer for them. And who merits this punishment more than the man who has caused your suffering?

The commonest cause of self-castigation is the realization that you have fallen for a Line or Technique, especially if it is one that has tripped you before, and more especially if you suspect you have been taken over by a Fly-by-Nighter. The best time to take the pleasure out of it for him is immediately after you become aware that you have made an error. And it is to be hoped that such awareness will come to you before he has said good-night —otherwise you may never hear from him again, which would deprive you of a chance to "get in your licks," as the saying goes.

Start Equalizing at once. The principle behind the Theory of Equalization is a simple one: the happier and more self-satisfied you know the man to be, the more

172

miserable you become. Conversely, as the man's pleasure decreases, your own increases, until you come out even— often obliterating all memory of your unhappiness.

Fortunately, a girl usually becomes conscious of her error in time, often recognizing it at the Point of No Return. Even though you cannot turn back, you can begin right then to prepare your revenge. A well-executed retaliation will serve to forestall or counteract the morning-after dejection, for you will wake up with the comforting knowledge that you have made him miserable, too.

First, it is terribly important not to let him see that he has made you unhappy. This would inflate his ego, and nothing makes a man happier than an inflated ego. Thus, you *in*crease instead of *de*crease his pleasure, and at that rate you will *never* catch up.

Second, do not "blame" him. This will gain you nothing—it will only antagonize him and make you seem petty. Instead, be as delightful as possible. Lull him into a false feeling of security—then when he is relaxed and self-satisfied, and perhaps a little tired—THEN—

Look at your watch—allow your attention to wander— smile absent-mindedly when he speaks—yawn (but daintily). Hasten the moment of parting, and then be unnecessarily polite as you say good-night. He will, of course, ask if anything is wrong. Do not give a direct answer. Be evasive, indifferent, aloof. Do not frown. Smile enigmatically, and send him on his way—puzzled and wounded.

If you despise yourself to an extraordinary degree, you may want to destroy him rather than merely wound him. In that event, your farewell can be quite different. Do not say much. Be laconic. Leave (or send him away) abruptly refusing to give any reasons, and ask him not to call you again.

If you can manage it, the ultimate insult is to ridicule

him. Laugh disparagingly at anything he does or says. Tell him with amused condescension that he needs a little more experience, or a little more talent, or a little more something—you know not what, but his embraces leave you cold. What more devastating accusation can be made against a man? And even if it is not true, you have planted in his mind the fear that perhaps it is. You have made him believe that in your eyes he looks ridiculous—and he will kick himself many times, which is a very nice substitute for kicking him yourself.

Generally speaking, a man is baffled by the woman who simultaneously gives herself and insults him. Your behaviour may so confound him that he will be impatient to see you again in order to solve the mystery. When he calls, you will have the pleasure of turning him down. Do so in a vague tentative way, so that he will call again—and again. Thus, before he realizes he is finished, you will be able to double or triple your enjoyment. And for weeks or months, maybe years, he will know the torment of an unsatisfied curiosity.

It is not only in a sudden association that one finds it necessary to take the pleasure out of it for him. A man you have known for some time may give evidence that he is unworthy, i.e., stingy or ungrateful or unfaithful. Under these circumstances, it is possible to use more elaborate means of torture, since you have time to prepare, to set the stage, as it were.

You should not, of course, let him suspect that you are offended. Do not sulk or pout or quarrel. Be your most charming. The wounds inflicted at a love-feast carry more sting than those exchanged in battle. The following suggestions are valuable only insofar as they indicate what direction to take. Knowing your man and his vulnerable areas, you will be able to create specific torments to suit the individual.

# HOW TO TAKE THE PLEASURE OUT OF IT

## *Some Ways To Make a Man Miserable*

### CALL HIM BY PET NAMES

In the midst of a beautiful embrace, whisper "Darling Tommy" in his ear—or "My Johnnie Boy" or "Oh, Dickie." This will freeze the muscles of his heart if his name happens to be George.

### GIVE HIM GIFTS

Buy him a pair of socks several sizes too large for him. When he tries them on, laugh with fond amusement, and say you never realized he was so little. (Naturally this can

be used only on small or medium-sized men.) You may carry this idea further according to your financial means. A huge sweater, or an enormous shirt, or tremendous gloves, or gigantic pyjamas can make a man dwindle away to nothing—and likewise his ego. For the man who is the least big pudgy, or putting on a little extra weight, reverse the procedure—buy him tiny garments.

## BE INTERESTED

But not in the things that interest him. Create a perfect setting, with soft lights and music—and after two or three kisses, start a conversation. Your voice should be clear and strong, and the subject a prosaic one—like the newest development in a comic strip, or how to remove ink stains. When the music stops, stop everything. Insist on silence while you listen to a radio talk. Or encourage him to talk about himself, and when he has warmed to his subject, pretend you have fallen asleep.

## BE ROMANTIC

Listen to the music with a dreamy, far-away look—and say it reminds you of something, but don't tell him what it is. Or talk admiringly about a man you know—or one you do not know, like an actor or some other public figure —praising his appearance, his mind, his personality. Or arrange with some girl to phone you. Pretend the call is from a man, call him darling, and giggle and coo a great deal. Or send yourself a box of flowers, card enclosed, and have them delivered while he is there. Then devote the major part of the evening to arranging them, finding the right spot for them, feeding them aspirin and salt, smelling them, rearranging them, and admiring them. Or tell him he reminds you of someone you used to know—he dances like someone you used to know—he makes love like someone you used to know. Comparisons are always painful.

## PLAY DEAD

Accept his kisses and caresses with lifeless passivity. Let yourself go limp all over, like a rag doll. As he frantically tries to elicit some reaction, remark that the room is chilly and go for a sweater.

## BE METICULOUS

Avoid his kisses entirely and offer him a chlorophyll tablet. Or have your hair done in some elaborate style and spend the evening protecting it. Warn him frequently not

to disarrange it, and every time he gains a little ground, pull away hastily. This is doubly effective if you hint that the special coiffure is for an important date the following night.

## BE OBSERVANT

Notice things about him. Notice how thin his hair has become, or how the hairline recedes. Notice how soft he is getting, or how his tummy is starting to bulge. Notice some grey hairs. Notice the crowsfeet on his eyebags. (Men are as sensitive as women about signs of approaching age.) But do not criticize—commiserate. And be kind. Tell him looks are not important—that he may be far from an Adonis, but you don't care what a man looks like, as long as he doesn't bore you. This is a good prelude to a series of yawns, or a little catnap.

So mortified will the average man be by the treatment described that he will never be heard from again. There are some fellows, though, who are thick-skinned and not so quick to take offence. With typical obtuseness this type will say to himself, "What's eating her?" or "She must be off her feed." And he will come back for a repeat performance before he disappears.

Whatever his reaction, immediate or delayed, it is a great comfort to know that you have cancelled out any pleasure he may previously have derived from you. In fact, an evening devoted to Equalizing, to making some deserving man miserable, can be so rewarding an experience that you may come through it happier than you were before you began to hate yourself.

## CHAPTER TWENTY

# On Catching
# a Wealthy Sponsor

THERE is a popular belief that any girl who is willing to "pay the price" can acquire a Wealthy Sponsor. *This is not true.* On the contrary, the snaring of such a man is a rare and delicate feat.

Entirely too many girls have the fantastic idea that all they need do is Give—and they will Receive. Ha! If it were as simple as that, we would all be wearing mink. How often have you heard some female say, "Oh, well! If I wanted to do that sort of thing, I could have furs and jewels and money in the bank, too." This is pure fantasy. There are thousands of girls who "do that sort of thing"— with very wealthy men—and never realize a penny profit.

 *And there are tens of thousands who, try as they may, cannot even attract the improper advances of a wealthy man!*

179

Actually, it is far more difficult to acquire a Sponsor than to catch a husband. To begin with, only three per cent of the male population is wealthy enough to qualify. Just think how many women are trying for each member of that select group. After you eliminate the unattractive women, the inexperienced, and the inadequate, the competition is still too much for any but the most gifted.

Even girls who are both talented and diligent frequently fail. For Luck plays an important role. So much depends on getting the breaks, on having the right contacts, on the accident of proper timing.

True, on rare occasions a novice who has none of the qualifications for success (and often no ambition) will by some quirk of chance be precipitated into a brilliant alliance with a rich man. Reports of this kind of accidental success give many naïve girls a false perspective on the Wealthy Sponsor situation, and they promptly fling themselves into the contest with great expectations and childish fancies. I sincerely hope you will not be one of those who rush in where angels fear to tread.

The man of wealth usually doles out his gifts, if not with reluctance, certainly without abandon. He is disinclined to share his gold with one who, for all he knows, may not even like him. It takes a very subtle diplomat, indeed, to convince such a man that she has no interest in his money, and at the same time get him to give it to her. The woman who can do this—who can lead him from perfume to pearls to real estate and finally to annuities—is endowed with qualities which would ensure a success in any career she chose. Fearless, resourceful, determined, imaginative, far-sighted—one cannot help but regret that she does not see fit to exploit her talents in more legitimate if less lucrative fields.

The ability to capture and exploit a rich lover is one of those inexplicable talents, a gift of the gods, which cannot be learned, imitated, or acquired. There are more failures

in this field than in any other field of endeavour a woman may enter. The intelligent girl can easily calculate how slight are her chances of success, and she will turn her back on this difficult way of life to settle for the comfort, convenience, and security of Marriage.

CHAPTER TWENTY-ONE

# Don't Have An Affair
# With Your Boss

WE all know how desirable it is to Marry the Boss. This is the prime ambition—and a worthy one—of nine-tenths of all single women who work for a living. Marry him, I say, by all or any means, but *Do Not Have an Affair with Him*. All affairs are deplorable, but this type is one of the worst. Whether you work in an office, a factory, a department store, or wherever—your boss, or your immediate superior, is an unfortunate choice for a lover. The reasons against such an alliance are numerous.

1. You are deprived of one of the nicest features of an affair—the sweetness of seeing only the best of each other in the few, never-enough, stolen hours. The palpitating heart, the adoring glance, the eager embrace—you can hardly expect these from a man who sees as much of you as your boss does.

2. Every morning you must leave your home as fastidiously groomed, as carefully dressed, as if you were on your way to a rendezvous. The strain of maintaining so high a degree of perfection can become most tiresome.

3. Your fellow workers will be jealous of you and will endeavour to make your working hours miserable.

4. You will be expected to take a personal interest in his business affairs. This means you will put in longer hours, take on added duties, and in general be obliged to work much harder than you would for a stranger.

5. You are vulnerable on two interlocking fronts, occupying the uncomfortable position of a woman who cannot risk offending her lover or antagonizing her boss. You may well wake up one sad morning, simultaneously bereft of both man and job.

6. It is bad, psychologically, to have for a lover someone you must defer to forty hours a week. A handicap of this kind is difficult to overcome, and you may never gain the ascendancy. He is apt to think less of you always as the "girl who works for him."

The lover/boss is a dual personality, with the lover side of him influencing the boss, and the boss side influencing the lover—always to your disadvantage. As your lover he will never give you a mink coat or a diamond wrist watch or a Daimler. He will buy you, instead, a beaver lamb jacket, a 9-carat gold wrist watch, and a Morris Minor— all of which the boss in him considers more appropriate for one in your economic and social position. As your boss, he cannot forget he is your lover, and he hesitates to advance your career. He feels obliged to bend over backward to avoid the appearance of favouring his sweetheart. He is determined to be fair, at no matter what cost to you.

"Really?" you will say. "But I know Miss A. or Miss B. or Miss C. who is vice-president of the Such-and-Such Corporation—and everyone knows how she got there."

Yes. Most of the talented and capable women who occupy prestige jobs were given help by some man. But such good fortune is not representative of the average case. Simple arithmetic must tell you that the odds are against you. The number of important positions open to women is

extremely small in comparison to the unlimited number of ambitious women who are having affairs with their bosses.

Actually you cannot count on gaining very much. You may at best hope for more frequent increases in salary, longer vacations, bigger bonuses, promotion preferment, and that is all. If you weigh these advantages against all the disadvantages, you will readily see in which direction your choice should lie, and you will make this your working motto:

Marry him if you can—and if you cannot, forego him!

184

CHAPTER TWENTY-TWO

# Don't Have An Affair
# With a Married Man

*"Be not made a beggar by banqueting upon borrowing."*
—APOCRYPHA

THE most unsatisfactory lover in the world is the man who has a wife. A liaison with him is encumbered with all the customary inconveniences of a love-affair, plus the irritation of having a rival who outranks you.

In every aspect of your relationship with him, you feel her influence. The very hours you spend with him are dictated by *her* tastes and *her* schedule. If she loves a gay social life, you can be sure her husband will seldom be at your disposal in the evening—you must content yourself with odd hours during the day. If she is the athletic type, it is unlikely you will ever get to go sailing, fishing, or golfing with him. Whatever her habits, you must at all times be prepared for the sudden cancellation of a carefully planned rendezvous and equally prepared for an unexpected message that he is free—just when it is least convenient for you.

> YOU SOON COME TO REALIZE THAT YOU ARE HAVING
> AN AFFAIR NOT WITH JUST A MAN, BUT WITH A MAN
> AND THE UBIQUITOUS SHADOW CAST BY HIS WIFE.

You have no choice but to zig when she zags, and zag
when she zigs. And heaven help you if she is a woman who
frequently changes her mind!

Of one thing you can be sure—your lover will not spend
Christmas, New Year, or Easter Sunday with you. All the
important dates on the calendar belong to his wife and
children, and you will be forced to celebrate with relatives
or female friends—a sad prospect for a lively girl. Manless
amid the festivities, you will look about indignantly at
other women proudly displaying their escorts.

When you do get together, your married beau, with
commendable caution, will rule out all the nice places to

which you ask to be taken, and you will pass the time tucked away in some little room or in your own apartment. This has the value of being economical as well as discreet —important considerations for a family man.

The most cogent argument against having an affair with someone else's husband, is that

 *Married men virtually never marry their girl friends.*

Men hate divorce. They dislike the nuisance of moving, and besides, they resent paying alimony. If a man can possibly endure his wife, he will stay married to her.

In any event, the fact that a man takes a sweetheart does not indicate that he prefers the sweetheart to his wife. Not at all. Ninety times out of a hundred he would be aghast at the idea of trading his good old wife for some wanton stranger.

Can any girl really be happy with the humble assignment of amusing a man who belongs to somebody else? I think not. Then what induces her to become part of such a makeshift arrangement?

I put this question to a number of women who are involved with married men. Most of them whimpered, "I didn't know he was married until it was too late."

Some, however, were quite unabashed. "There are not enough good men to go around," they explained . . . "All the best ones are taken. . ." And they "would rather scrimp along on a fragment of some superior male than own an ordinary one outright and in his entirety."

A handful of girls confessed they were lazy and rather than try for a single man, they chose to eke what pleasure they could from the more easily acquired married one. Such lack of ambition is lamentable. I am glad to report that the average girl considers her married lover but a stopgap and is constantly on the lookout, hoping to better herself.

There was one girl, however, who claimed she actually preferred sharing some other woman's husband to having one of her own. "A wife," she declared, "has the burden of taking care of his household and his petty needs. To her fall the menial tasks of seeing to his socks and his shirts, his meals and his stomach aches, and all the other drab day-to-day chores of making him comfortable. Happy and well-fed he comes to me for his lighter hours. I get the best of him—the playmate, the sweetheart, the lover."

Obviously this is a rationalization. In her heart of hearts every woman longs for the socks and the shirts. If you settle for less, you will always feel cheated.

## CHAPTER TWENTY-THREE

# How Shall We Love Them?

THESE studies, which deal with the period between a girl's adolescence and her marriage, emphasize, perforce, the superior position of the male. But one must not lose sight of the fact that this pre-marital period, when the balance of power is in man's favour, is short-lived. The ultimate triumph is ours. For once man is caught in marriage, the inequality shifts. Poor John! *He* is the one who is put upon and taken advantage of—and never again does he attain the status of a free human being—unless he is fortunate enough, or desperate enough, to achieve widowerhood.

It is the knowledge of what awaits him that provokes man to employ the time of his youth and desirability to bedevil women and deceive them and defy them; he has but one way of evening the score and he uses it to the hilt. This is the only time in her life that a woman is more or less powerless. She cannot use force to make him legally hers—and she cannot turn her back on him, as each man is a potential husband. She can only be philosophic, treat all men gently, and WAIT—secure in the knowledge that she will have a life-long revenge from the day she becomes a bride. (It is a mistake, of course, to think of marriage

189

merely as an instrument of retaliation. That is but one of the minor benefits to be enjoyed.)

Matrimony is woman's greatest glory, a shining monument to her ingenuity and will-power. She has managed to domesticate and enslave that unruly beast called **Man,**

even though he is bigger and stronger and smarter than she is. We have a tendency to gloat over this remarkable achievement and exult because Man is under our dominion from birth to adolescence and from marriage to the grave.

BUT—in celebrating these victories, we ignore that embarrassing hiatus between adolescence and marriage. Why have we never developed an impenetrable defence against man's impositions during his free-lance period?

It is not too late to correct this oversight. And it should be corrected. If we bring men to heel in the one last carefree period left to them, we shall then have completely subordinated the entire sex, leaving no loophole to weaken our position.

To do this we must unite. With strong wills and singleness of purpose we must make a solemn pact to deny ourselves as a body to all men who seek to obtain at no cost that for which they should pay with their lives.

How frantically then would they scurry about, searching for the last weak sisters—and how bewildered they would be as they were denied entrance at every door. In anguish they would turn away and cry out for the good old days. And finally, driven by their uncontrollable need for female companionship, they would all be forced to enter the divine state of Matrimony. For

 *Men cannot live without us.*

They need us with a need that cannot be denied, overcome or ignored. And it is this great masculine weakness which provides us with a weapon of infinite power. Let us learn to wield this weapon with feminine grace and tact. Let us be delectable and inaccessible and artful, but at the same time let us be kind.

For despite the fact that man is a predatory beast with the inherent cruelty of a small boy and the emotional stability of a weather-cock—despite the fact that he is baffling, unpredictable and demanding—despite all that can be said against him—he is nevertheless better than anything else yet created or invented for the pleasure of a woman.

Therefore let us overlook his imperfections. Nothing,

after all, is without fault. Do we not accept life with all its evils, its disappointments, and its indignities? Even so—as life is worth living

 *Men are worth loving.*